MW01048411

BOOK SIX

CHANGED LIVES

Ten True Stories: From Addiction to Freedom

Compiled by
PASCO A. MANZO

Foreword by Jerry Nance, Ph.D.
President/CEO – Global Teen Challenge

Changed Lives (Book Six)
Ten True Stories: From Addiction to Freedom
Compiled by Pasco A. Manzo

COPYRIGHT © 2019 by Teen Challenge New England, Inc.

Teen Challenge New England, Inc.
1311 Main Street
Brockton, MA 02301

All rights reserved. No part of this work may be reproduced or transmitted in any form or by any means, electronic or mechanical, including photocopying and recording, or by any information storage or retrieval system, except for brief quotations embodied in critical articles or reviews, without the permission in writing from the copyright owner. For information, email info@tcnewengland.org or write to Teen Challenge New England, Inc., 1311 Main Street, Brockton, MA 02301.

All Scripture quotations are taken from the Holy Bible, New International Version® unless otherwise noted. NIV®. Copyright © 1973, 1978, 1984 by International Bible Society, Zondervan Bible Publishers.

Edited by Brian Dube and Mary Ann Manzo
Jacket and Layout Design by Eric Castonguay

ISBN: 978-0-578-54458-8

Printed in the United States of America
2019 - First Edition

Dedication

This book is dedicated to the memory of our dear friend Mayor Bill Carpenter. Mayor Carpenter served the city of Brockton, MA from 2014 - 2019 and was an ardent supporter of Teen Challenge New England & New Jersey.

For each of these past five years, Mayor Carpenter was one of the first people to be presented a copy of Changed Lives.

Book Six is here Mayor!

"For God is not unjust. He will not forget your work and the love you have shown Him as you have helped His people."
Hebrews 6:10

Contents

Back Page Contents

Foreword

Jerry Nance, Ph.D.
President/CEO
Global Teen Challenge

The ministry of Teen Challenge witnesses life transformation on a daily basis in over 1,400 locations in 125 nations of the world. With over 60 years of experience providing hope to the hopeless, Teen Challenge leaders continue to trust God for miracles in the lives of each and every person who walks through our doors.

It is such a joy to read these wonderful testimonies of how God's grace has impacted the lives of broken people through the ministry of Teen Challenge New England and New Jersey. One story after another provides layer after layer of hope for the reader. If you know anyone who is struggling with addiction, buy them a copy of this book! In fact, I would encourage you to buy multiple copies and allow these testimonies to bring hope to those who read them.

Around the world we have continued to see the death toll rise from addiction. In 2017, more than 72,000 individuals died from drug overdoses, with over 50% of those being from opioids. This is one of the most critical health issues facing America today. However, there is hope and it is found in the life changing power of Jesus Christ.

The powerful work of this ministry is effective no matter the culture. Teen Challenge is operating in every region of the world. Teen Challenge ministries can be found across Africa, Europe, Eurasia, North and South America, Northern and Southern Asia, and the Asia Pacific. There are over 20,000 individuals in residential care and more than 250,000 in outpatient programs.

I want to applaud the work of Pasco Manzo and all of the team at Teen Challenge New England and New Jersey, for making these powerful testimonies possible and available to share. As they work to Give Hope to Addicts and Families, these personal stories of freedom are a real encouragement for anyone still struggling.

Introduction: Short and Long-Term Residential Care

Bob Gallagher, Director
Massachusetts TC Clinical Group, LICSW
Joe Rand, Director Teen Challenge Massachusetts

This chapter will provide information and an overview of both the short and long- term treatment options available through Teen Challenge to help those individuals struggling with substance use disorder. At Teen Challenge, we believe that at the core of any lasting recovery is a personal relationship with Jesus Christ. It has always been the desire of Teen Challenge to offer that hope to the most amount of people possible. The individuals seeking our help come from a wide variety of backgrounds and find themselves in very different circumstances surrounding their addiction. Therefore, there is considerable benefit in our ability to offer a variety of treatment options in response. Bob Gallagher, LICSW is the Director of the new Massachusetts TC Clinical Group. In that role, Bob oversees and will explain the short-term treatment options. Joe Rand, Director of Teen

Challenge Massachusetts (Brockton), will explain the long-term or "Legacy" program.

Short-Term Treatment

There are different short-term treatment options for substance use disorder and the commonly co-existing mental health issues. Here at Teen Challenge New England and New Jersey we will soon be opening two such programs. The first of these programs is Acute Treatment Services (ATS), which is also known as detoxification or "detox." The detox program can last anywhere from 4-14 days depending on the needs of the patient and their treatment follow-through. The next short-term program is known as Clinical Stabilization Services (CSS), which is often known as "step-down." This program typically will last from 7-14 days but in some circumstances it may last as many as 30 days. The specifics of these two treatment options will be discussed in a later chapter. This chapter will explore the overall benefits and limitations of short-term programs.

There are two primary benefits to short-term treatment for individuals with substance use disorder. They are the two most important. First, it is life preserving. That is to say that the goal of the initial engagement, whether that be by medical personnel, law enforcement or a program clinician is to preserve life. Any long-term recovery must begin with a medical assessment and physical separation from the substance being abused. Only after this takes place can the second benefit happen which is having the individual in an environment where a seed to recovery and lasting change can be planted. There is much truth to the adage, "A dead addict cannot recover." If an individual loses their life, they cannot change and grow into the person they were meant to be.

The beginnings of short-term treatment; the initial assessment and sometimes detoxification is often done at a hospital and then the goal of finding proper placement begins. The next positive aspect of short-term programming is that hopefully, now that the individual has been stabilized, the seed of recovery has been planted. A treatment team is entrusted to care for and assist the person as they move on to the next step of their recovery. This seed could come from a particular group or individual session that deeply connects with a person or could be something the person reads or hears someone else share. Treating an individual who is suffering with substance use disorder with compassion, dignity and respect will help that person see their worth and give them hope to progress forward in their journey towards sobriety and a joyful life. Most of the people that come through our doors have little self-worth. Showing care for the person goes a long way towards planting that seed and opening their eyes to the potential to real recovery. Having appropriate personal connections in a short-term program benefit the individual being cared for as well as the caregivers by allowing for growth in compassion and understanding. Throughout my 28 years in the human services profession, I have continued to grow through each interaction I have with those I serve, as well as with my staff and colleagues.

Though there are several benefits to short-term programs, there are limits as well. Some limitations immediately evident are too brief a period of interaction or a quick turn-around. It often takes more time than 30 days to change a behavior. We see individuals who are in the midst of active abuse and lasting change takes time. The result is that we often see the same people continuously cycle in and out of treatment. These people do not stay long enough for the seed of change to be planted in such a way to allow it to take root and grow. Instead, they come in for a few days of detox and then they get an urge and instead of continuing in treatment, go out again to use their substance of choice.

To show both sides of this and how it can turn positive, I will use an example from my past. I worked with a young man several years ago who was a person who did this on a regular basis. I would see him often at two different programs I operated and after a while I took him aside and asked him why he never tried to go further in supervised treatment if he really wanted to change. His answer the first time I asked him is one I never forgot. He said, "If I kept going in treatment I would not know if they would take care of me Bob, I know you guys will." This was a great compliment to the people he worked with but also something nice to say to the director to try to get me to back off a bit. He was someone who was truly in the grips of his addiction. The good part was he kept making it back when a lot of people he used with did not. Two years later at a more recent placement I directed, he was referred to us and I overruled a hold order placed by a previous director due to the frequency of visits. After a couple of days he and I met. He was surprised to see me and even more surprised I remembered our conversation from two years previous. I assured him it struck me as honest and a touch of telling me what I wanted to hear and I asked him which it was and what is different now. He said, "I remember Bobby G and I meant it, you and your people were always respectful and seemed to give a darn (alteration)." His answer to what is different now was "As for now, I had close to a year sober recently because I finally thought I mattered and then my daughter came back to my life then she od'd and I have been going since, so what is different "I have no one." During our discussion I asked, "Why are you here instead of just continuing your current use pattern?" He had no good answer except that he didn't know. He went to an ER and then came here. We talked for a bit more and decided to talk every other day while he was here. The days we did not talk he spoke with his case manager and attended groups. For the first time, he stayed in treatment to completion. He then went on to further treatment for the first time ever. For him, the "no one" feeling worked for his recovery. He was ready for the seed to be planted and flourish. For others the state he was in could have done the complete opposite direction. I chose this example to show a good outcome for someone who was ready even though he did not realize he was, and how the people can not only be the seed but often are the seed themselves for those entrusted to our care.

Unfortunately, the above true story is one that is few and far between. The majority of "frequent fliers" do not get the seed to grow and often the people we read about or that are in treatment programs are the names and/or pictures we put on a memorial wall for those who are lost to addiction before they were able to get the grace to beat it.

Short-term programs are a great way to get quick help and for some that is enough to change the choices they are making. Long-term programs like short-term ones vary in time, style, approach, etc. There is a lot of literature stating that it takes anywhere from three to six months to change a behavior or habit and make it part of their new routine. Joe will discuss the long-term, Legacy Program we offer here at

Teen Challenge and how it has been and continues to be incredibly successful for those helped.

Long-Term Treatment

Teen Challenge New England and New Jersey has existed for over 50 years. During that time we have used the model of a long-term, faith-based residential recovery program. Currently, the long-term adult program is a 12 to 15 month program. We have found over the years of using this model that there are many benefits and that the success rate rises as residents complete the full program. This first part of this chapter will highlight the model we use and its benefits as well as some of the struggles and why we have added a short-term option.

We are now calling our long-term model our Legacy Program. There is very little data that is current that supports one model of recovery over another. There is a study that is being worked on now that is collecting that data and will help us compare recovery models and their successes. The last study completed has success rates of long-term Teen Challenge centers on 86%, which is far higher than any other program or model. We have found that working with individuals for a long time gives us the opportunity to help them not only with their addiction issues, but also with the character issues that surface when the substances are removed. A long-term model provides many benefits that due to their very nature, short-term programs cannot.

The Legacy Program is a five-phase program with each phase lasting three months. Here is the breakdown of each phase with goals for each.

Phase 1 - To acquaint the new resident with the Teen Challenge philosophy, rules and regulations.

Phase 2 - To establish the resident in the foundations of the Christian faith, and to begin the discipleship process.

Phase 3 - To give the maturing resident further practical opportunities to use the biblical principles taught in Phase 1.

Phase 4 - To give the maturing resident an atmosphere where he can continue to apply the principles learned in Phase 2 while assisting staff in their duties.

Phase 5 - To make the transition from resident to graduate, and to implement their Aftercare Plan. This plan is FUTURE FOCUSED! We are committed to helping build a solid foundation for each resident's future so they can succeed in life. This includes vocational/educational goals, finding and maintaining a stable and healthy living situation, and becoming a committed part of a local church.

One of the special things about our Legacy Program

is that you are living day by day with individuals that are in the same structure and rules as you are, that come from the same background as you do, but they are all at different steps in their recovery. From day one to the end of month 15, as well as graduates that are now in the apprenticeship program or on staff, you are living alongside people that are on the same journey as you are. It can be very encouraging to meet someone who was in your same situation only weeks or months earlier and has found victory. It can also be very encouraging to find out a staff member, whom you would never guessed struggled with addiction, was also in your very same situation. This can provide hope where there was hopelessness. It also allows for some intense discipleship because you are rubbing shoulders with these individuals all day and they are showing you a better way to do things. There is a special bond that is forged between staff and residents because of the care, patience, and determination of staff. Although many are not formally trained, they have walked in the shoes of the resident and can relate to them so well.

Research suggests that it can take up to 254 days for a routine to become a habit. During that time of creating a habit, it is important to have reminders. Nightly Bible reading is a good example of this. Part of the schedule each night is to read your Bible. We do this at the same time, in the same place, each night. Early on, residents need to be reminded of this task and its importance. Eventually it becomes a routine but it is still not a habit. A habit does not form until you start seeing the rewards that come from that routine. In this case, the reward is you are having your mind washed clean of the wrong ways of thinking and allow your mind to be made new. When temptation comes or you are struggling with a circumstance, the Word of God is brought to your mind and you reap the rewards of your routine. Now you are equipped with a habit that will help you have continued success when you graduate and leave the program.

Another benefit of long-term is that you experience more real life situations with a safety net to help you though them. A lot can happen in 12 to 15 months and it is important to have support around you. Because of the length of the program, we can dedicate the final three months to re-entry, which allows for this support system and safety net to be transferred to family, church, and friends.

It may not take a full year for someone to be free from substances and addiction but the truth is, that is when the real work begins. Life after substances is hard because you are confronted with all of the things you were using substances to avoid and more importantly, you are confronted with yourself. You can ride the "pink cloud" for a little while and you may be able to fake it for a couple months, but being in a long-term program, you will eventually be confronted with your issues. By addressing the moral and character issues in your life, you have the ability to break free from the idea that you will always be an addict. As the residents begin to identify as a child of God instead of an addict, they are empowered to make real and lasting changes in their life.

Usually by the time someone enters Teen Challenge, they have burned bridges with family and friends that would be assets in the recovery process. Instead, most have replaced those relationships with negative influences that will enable the addict to continue. By being in a long term program, the residents of Teen Challenge are able to show their family and friends that they are sincere about changing their behaviors and that they are committed to getting and staying off of substances. Likewise, the time they spend in the residential program helps break them away from the negative influences and unhealthy relationships. Many times life-long friendships are formed because of what the residents have gone through together.

Residents of Teen Challenge are not only having their relationships with family restored, but they are learning how to have positive interactions with everyone around them. Living in a residential program in dorm style conditions has a way of bring those issues up quickly so you are able to deal with them. Some need to learn the social skills needed to live

21

with others and some need a refresher on these skills but for everyone, it is an important step for long-term success because you will always be around people and learning how to navigate different relationships can help you avoid a relapse down the road.

Teen Challenge also offers a vocational component in the Legacy Program. You begin to work in different areas of the program. Some help prepare and serve the meals, some work on building maintenance or landscaping, and some may help fundraise. Through all of this vocational training, it teaches the residents work ethic and practical skills to be a productive member of society when they graduate the program. It serves a secondary purpose as well by helping bring in funds to help cover the cost to bring in more residents. This helps give residents purpose. While they are in the program to work on their own lives, they are helping others at the same time.

Another benefit to long-term treatment as opposed to short-term option is the cost to the resident and their families. Because Teen Challenge is not a medical facility that has doctors and nurses on staff, this lowers the cost per resident in the program. This allows residents to remain in the program without incurring a financial burden. And while they are not allowed to get a job and earn money, all of their needs are being met while they are there.

Through all of the training received in the Legacy Program of Teen Challenge, residents leave ready to live successful lives without drugs and alcohol. They are also prepared to have healthy relationships, be solid employees, and be involved in their local church.

Our combination of the Detox Acute Treatment Services (ATS), short-term Clinical Stabilization Services (CSS), and long-term Legacy programs on our Brockton, Massachusetts campus brings a fully comprehensible approach offering the best of solutions available today for substance use disorder and the addiction epidemic affecting so many thousands of people in society, many of whom are in our own personal worlds. We are ready, willing, and waiting to help all and any one who reaches out for that help today.

Chapter 1
Massachusetts TC Clinical Group

Bob Gallagher, LICSW

A new clinical component has been added to the treatment options offered by Teen Challenge New England and New Jersey. These services are being offered at the Massachusetts center located in Brockton, Massachusetts. The new entity is called Massachusetts TC Clinical Group and within it are three new programs: Outpatient (which opened in December 2018), Short-term/Clinical Stabilization Services (CSS) opened in the fall of 2019, and the Acute Treatment Services (ATS/Detox) which will be opening in the winter of 2020.

These programs are being offered as additional options to complement our long-term program in order to help more individuals and families dealing with substance use disorder. This will be accomplished by continuing to focus on our core values of integrity, excellence, service, and leadership. The continuum of detox, CSS, short-term and outpatient will add to the existing long-term, faith-based Legacy Program thus creating a continuum of care in one location. Having all of these options offered at one site will add to the quality of services for those entrusted to us for support. It will help us be considered as an option for those who cannot enter into a long-term program for a variety of reasons.

The continuum is often initiated at an emergency room or another placement program. An individual requires services due to recent issues, such as an overdose or legal issues brought on by using/abusing drug or alcohol. The person goes to an ER at a local hospital and gets assessed to find the proper placement. If it is determined that the person needs medical inpatient acute care services to for their physical safety during the withdrawal management phase of care, then this necessitates a referral to a detox. This determination is made based on a set of criteria with the wellbeing of the patient given priority. The first placement for these individuals is detox or medically (and clinically) monitored withdrawal management as defined by the American Society of Addiction Medicine (ASAM) criteria.

The detox level is a medical model of treatment which is overseen by a nurse manager and medical director. There is a team of nurses, case managers, and direct care staff (called recovery specialists or RS's) that assist people in this phase.

It is at this time when people are at their most vulnerable. They are monitored closely to deal with their withdrawal symptoms and each person is placed on a medical protocol to deal with their symptoms.

Team communication is of utmost importance because of any of the physical issues that present in the patients at the detox level. It is vital that all of this information needs to go to the nursing staff. The RS's are the staff that spend the most time with oversight of the patients and must record and report to case management and nursing anything that may be of a concern. Daily notes and formal and informal shift meetings are vital in this process so that everyone is on the same page in assisting each patient on a daily/hourly/momentary basis. The case managers under the supervision of the clinical director are responsible for individual check-ins and full sessions with each patient along with facilitating all required groups at the detox level mandated by the Bureau of Substance Abuse Services (BSAS) regulations. These groups cover, but are not limited to such topics as: medication assisted treatment (MAT), relapse prevention, early recovery, peer supports, and aftercare options. The case managers are also the ones responsible to facilitate the aftercare for each member on their respective caseloads. The aftercare could be transitioning to our CSS or to a different facility, or perhaps to our outpatient services or one at another location, or could include returning to their jobs and homes. Aftercare is often unique, and the case manager must look into a myriad of options. Patients can be at the ATS or detox level anywhere from 4 to 14 days depending on the individual level of need as defined by the ASAM, which is the criteria used in determining placement and follow through. The longer the person stays the better their outcome can be. This is because they are healthier and further from the event or chain of events that led them into treatment. They are better able to look at options and they can hopefully better focus on themselves. This is one of the strengths of the next level of care on the continuum, CSS.

This next level of care of the short-term program is Clinical Support Services (CSS). The CSS level is less of a medical treatment. There is medical follow through at this level, but not like at the detox level. The clients are in a more stable, safer, manageable state and can be monitored by nursing on a more periodic basis and more by observation from the clinical and residential staff. At the Massachusetts TC Clinical Group short-term program there will be 36 client beds with an average length of stay between 14-30 days. The men being served there will have access to a program nurse 30 hours per week with emergency access 24 hours a day from the nursing team at the detox including the nurse manager for the three new clinical programs. At the CSS level clients will attend six groups a day for seven days a week and meet with a clinician three times a week for a 45-60 minute session each time. The groups are a combination of clinician led and staff led groups. The clinician led groups are didactic (classroom style) in nature and the expectations and goals of each group will be outlined so the clients and facilitator are working towards those goals on a consistent basis. The sharing of information is designed to help the people being served gain strength to aid them in making better choices to enhance their lives and therefore their recovery. There will also be some activity-based groups that could be led by a clinician, case manager, RS, peer, or guest presenter. In this program the client's focus is on getting emotionally and clinically stronger so they can move onward in their journey of recovery. The movement could be to further treatment through the Legacy Program (The name for the long-term Teen Challenge option) or to a different long-term placement. The movement could also be back to the environment the person came from, such as their home, with an outpatient provider to assist in the next phase of the journey. The tools and support they receive stay with them as they continue on.

Each of these levels have a structured curriculum that the groups follow. There are many curricula that programs follow at all levels of care. The one we have chosen to use is Helping Men Recover. This is an evidence-based curriculum with a spiritual offering that is both a requirement of BSAS in

CSS programs. It also provides a good opportunity to help assess if the Legacy Program may be the correct option at this time in their journey or if another setting is a more proper fit. We will offer a group in our short-term program based on spirituality. This will be an optional group for the people to choose from among the many other groups offered during their stay. The literature in evidence-based practices does support the need for and importance of spiritual connections for short-term and long-lasting recovery. What the research does not support is one spiritual style over another. This supports the approach we will be taking at Massachusetts TC Clinical Group throughout our programs.

The third of our new programs is called Outpatient. The outpatient program has begun as outpatient services for the men served here in our Legacy Program as well as people in the greater Brockton community. This service began in December of 2018. We currently provide group therapy to our residents on Monday and Tuesday evenings and individual counseling to adolescents and adults from Brockton and neighboring towns during the weekdays. The evening groups are facilitated by a licensed clinician and the clients that attend them are assured of confidentiality and safety in the group. The group ranges from five to ten participants. Keeping the group at this range gives everyone an opportunity to be active in the group and feel a sense of connection with the facilitator and each other different from the ways they connect outside of group therapy.

Individual counseling helps those with substance use disorder and other mental health disorders such as bipolar, anxiety, depression, PTSD, and borderline personality disorder. All of these concerns are supported in the most caring and compassionate manner for those that have come to us and who deserve our best at all times. As the outpatient program grows, we will be offering an Intensive Outpatient Program (IOP). What makes it intensive is the amount of groups and individual sessions required. This is for people transitioning from a higher level of care, often either detox or CSS, or those that need structure to assist in their focus on change and recovery. The outpatient services are also offered in conjunction with or in lieu of some of the other continuum options. There are some insurance providers that will not pay for residential supports for the members even though these supports are the correct support for the person at that time. It is easier and less expensive to provide Outpatient Services and have the person get less than the prescribed care he/she requires/deserves in order to provide the best quality for the person being served. This is why we will be adding IOP to our options here at Massachusetts TC Clinical Group. Outpatient providers are therefore often taxed with helping people that are in a challenging stage of their recovery and often are not

Changed Lives

equipped to support the person suffering in front of them in the moment. At Massachusetts TC Clinical Group, we have the resources to support these individuals due to having all members of the continuum of care in one location.

A way to show how someone may pass through the continuum is to discuss the example of Chris H. Chris H. has been addicted to heroin for six years and has been in 12 detoxes over the past two years all with the same result. He goes in, gets a few days of safe and clean time, and goes out and uses within five days of discharge. He has only gone to further treatment once four years ago when he went from detox to a TSS (transitional support services) and then to a reputable sober house without any counseling or work while there. He was able to stay sober for almost one full year going through this path. There were a couple of stops he missed. Let us pretend to walk Chris H. through the continuum of care at Massachusetts TC Clinical group.

Chris H. recently overdosed and was revived by Narcan from the Quincy police. Narcan is an opiate blocker that is administered nasally with two or more direct squeezes to revive the person from an opiate overdose. They then drove him to a hospital emergency room where he was tended to by Nurse Jane. Jane along with the team at her hospital convinced Chris to go to detox. Jane had case manager Tom reach out to Massachusetts TC Clinical Group and spoke with

John the Admissions Coordinator who performed the initial screening and accepted the referral after a quick discussion with the intake nurse Deb. The ambulance then drove Chris H. to 1315 Main Street Brockton for detox. Chris H. was able to complete his intake including his initial physical and urine. He was then shown his room and allowed to rest. He was then escorted to the nurse's station where he discussed his protocol choices with the floor nurse and the medical director via phone consultation. The decision was made to use the Suboxone protocol instead of the Methadone protocol due to Chris H.'s distaste of/allergic reaction to Methadone when put on the Methadone clinic in Boston several years ago. He took his Suboxone correctly and attended all required groups after day three. During the first two and a half days he was given medical approval to miss several group sessions due to being sick (a common occurrence the first couple of days in detox). He was able to complete his protocol on day nine and he showed his readiness for the next level of care. On day 10 he transitioned to the Massachusetts TC Clinical Group short-term program. The search for placement included other programs as well that Chris H. has known of but the decision was made to stay within the Massachusetts TC system. While at CSS Chris H. was followed medically by the nurse manager and the CSS nurse for med compliance and effectiveness of current medication. Chris H. was uncomfortable at first in some groups and particularly with individual counseling while at CSS. This is/was a common for Chris H. and often the reason why he did not go on to further treatment. He would attend all groups but was not his usual active self. When his counselor, a long time veteran supporting those with addiction and co-occurring issues, spoke with him as an equal and not as a "damaged, beaten, pile of rubble" (Chris H.'s words), he was very surprised. This was the first time in treatment that he felt people were good to him and cared about him and not just cared for him because it was their job. During their many talks, neither described them as sessions although they were; Chris H. became more comfortable with the process and talked about recovery and reconnected with his family.

These talks led to Chris to wanting further support. For the first time he was initiating this part of the discussion. Chris H. had completed his protocol follow up and his other medication and wanted to attend all offered groups not just the mandatory ones. It was the spirituality group covered in the Helping Men Recover curriculum that made him want to "check out" the Connecting With/To the Light group offered on Wednesday night. He was initially uncomfortable because he had moved away from all faith-based parts of his life years ago. His counselor was the co-facilitator of the group and introduced him to the other facilitator.

After the group, Chris H. asked to speak to the clinical

director about his aftercare plan. He wanted to attend the Legacy Program and grow closer to the feeling he "was receiving from those around this place." He was reminded to discuss with the counselor and aftercare coordinator first. He followed protocol and then discussed with clinical director regarding the Legacy Program. After the discussion, he was able to meet with an intern from the Legacy Program to discuss in detail. He was accepted but was unable to attend due to a family issue that required him to be unable to commit to 15 months at this time. The decision was to have him attend the outpatient program and continue to be part of the TC community. He attended the IOP and went to morning prayer and was also invited to have lunch with the other men of the long-term program. Chris H. was a vocal and focused member and often went on and took part in different ministry opportunities while in outpatient. The team helped him create a hybrid program that worked for him, the program, and his family. He also attended individual counseling and two group therapies as part of this plan. This hybrid approach shows that client-centered focus and how that helps individuals and the community. This hybrid would not have been as possible without having all parts of the continuum on the same property in Brockton.

The story of Chris H is one that has not happened yet. Chris H is based on someone I worked with who has been through several systems and did benefit when someone dealt with him as a person and not just an issue. The hypothetical example shows the continuum and how having all components at one location can help a struggling individual in his life journey. At Massachusetts TC Clinical Group each client/patient will be treated in this manner and know they are cared about and not just cared for.

Chapter 2
Joy

Henry Gernhardt

I remember Nightmute.

Snow was on the ground and the stairs were freshly painted. The paint was gray. I can't remember the game I was playing, but I remember noticing as I hid under the stairs that the top of my hood brushed the wet paint on the underside of the tread. Sure enough there was a stain. Dad would be angry with me.

I remember Princeton.

Grandma's house was just down the path. Dad had built a three-decker bunkbed for us kids—I got the top bunk. I remember enjoying Nova, Buck Rogers, The Muppet Show, and looking at the sun through Dad's telescope. I taught myself BASIC. I read a lot. I started school in first grade. I didn't really the kids around me. I went through my first two grades of school in one year.

I remember Huntington.

I didn't understand the social issues I was facing. I was a year and a half younger than my classmates, and also quicker to learn than most of them. Adolescence came late as compared to my peer group. Fitting in never happened.

But college did.

I remember my first college party.

I had found the misfits, the geeks, the sci-fi enthusiasts, the fandomites. With them I fit in. With them I could connect. I could brain dive into a subject and be guaranteed to find someone in the group who geeked out on the same thing.

The party was a simple birthday affair.

That came with vodka.

To this day I don't know how much I drank. I simply remember the drunk. I remember the loosening of inhibition. I remember being able to talk more freely. I remember laughing a lot. I remember feeling pleasure in the state. I remember knowing, in the back of my mind, that this was behavior of which my father would not approve. I remember walking in the house, being greeted, and simply reporting that I was going to bed. I remember uncharacteristically bumping into a doorframe on my way to my room.

And the next morning I was fine.

Life went... Interesting.

I met the woman who was to be my first wife. We

40

connected over a kiss. We spent a lot of time talking. We fell in love with each other. We began living together. We married. She didn't talk to me about my drinking. My days were sober. My time at work was sober. My time at school was sober. At parties or after she went to bed, however, the alcohol would come out.

And it was never just one drink.

It never had been just one drink.

It was never about just one drink.

The drink was the vehicle for the drug. For the buzz. For the potent feeling of the early drunk. And then, when the early drunk had moved into the true drunk, for the drunker.

We moved to central Kentucky, still college students, now expecting our daughter. My drinking was still relegated to evenings. Once our daughter came it seemed I was able to give the drinking a break—but only when they were at the house.

I wasn't the husband my then-wife needed. But there was enough blame to go around. I was disillusioned with the marriage and disillusioned with parenthood. Circumstances were such that I felt as if I wasn't *permitted* to be a father to my daughter. I struck up an affair with a woman at school.

And left my wife for her.

Time passed. I left school. My grandmother on my mother's side passed and I was given her Reader's Digest

Bible. My girlfriend and I got jobs at a horse boarding and training facility. One of our co-workers was a Christian.

It seemed strange how I wound up coming to Christ. I had been reading the Reader's Digest Bible—abridged and modified though it was—and was finding the subject matter interesting. A chance encounter with our Christian co-worker's church bulletin led me to ask her about her faith. She was visibly excited. She told me of her faith and of her church.

The following Sunday I went.

I was quite taken aback by the number of people greeting me. It was a strange thing. And the only thing I seemed to have in common with them was this... Desire. A desire to learn more about who Christ is, about who God is. A desire that was deeper even than that. I couldn't put my finger on it.

But yet, by November of 2000, I knew it was time.

I was baptized into the faith by a senior elder of the church, his wife and the church pastor bearing witness. I arose shaking, *knowing* something had changed, but unsure *what*.

My new girlfriend and I got married. At that time I didn't have even the first conceptualization of Godly submission. Again came a resurgence of drinking.

She tried to get me to stop. She tried to limit me. She tried everything she could to keep me from being the drunk I had become—but she couldn't find the key. And after four and a half years of marriage she felt she simply couldn't rebuild trust in me. And so we separated.

In 2006 I found myself—for the first time in my life—living alone. I quickly found that alcohol was my best friend. My life devolved to waking up, going to work still shaking, coming home, drinking, passing out. Lather, rinse, repeat.

Lather, rinse repeat.

Lather, rinse repeat.

Lather, rinse…

"God, **get me out of this!**"

Drunk and on my knees I cried out to God. I'd had it. It was enough. There was no way I was going to be able to get out of this on my own. I needed Him to get me out of the situation. I needed *Him* to make me better.

My prayers were answered quickly.

In retrospect it felt like God simply picked me up and placed me in Massachusetts. It was a bit more involved than that logistically, but so many things fell into place so easily that there was no other explanation.

By the end of December 2007 I was living in Brockton, Massachusetts. My brother gave me a job doing e-commerce development. I was enjoying life as I dove into the alphabet soup of languages that is the web development stack. I was enjoying church as I joined up with the Vineyard in Kingston,

Massachusetts.

But the drinking never went away.

The business closed and I found myself drunk and in dire straits. There was a week in February of 2009 during which the only time I left the apartment was to find more alcohol. My brother had checked in on me a couple of times only to find me drunk. He was concerned. My mother was concerned. My father was concerned.

And it was then I was told about Teen Challenge.

On March 6, 2009 I walked through the big glass doors at 20 Clifton Avenue in Brockton, Massachusetts. A big guy named José beamed a smile at me, greeted me warmly with a hug and said, "Welcome home." An animated fellow by the name of Johnny Wilsey came down the stairs, greeted me, ushered me into a room where I filled out what felt like reams of paperwork.

"Welcome to the army of the Lord," Johnny told me with a handshake as I signed the final paper.

Thirty days passed. When I was granted my first phone call I asked my brother to bring my clarinet and some new reeds. I began to play it. I was invited onto the worship team. I rediscovered the joy of music. And I discovered an amazing thing: It was easy to connect with the guys here. *This was no small thing.*

Never before had I found myself in an environment

44

where I felt *understood.* Never before had I had such exposure to so many different walks of life in one place. Never before had I had such an opportunity to learn not only intellectually, but socially, emotionally, and spiritually.

It was truly a Godsend.

Of course, it was not without its challenges. There were rules to follow. There were things I was required to do as part of the program that I simply didn't want to do. Despite my desire to remain a simple follower, I was expected to lead. I had to learn what leadership *was.* I surprised myself as I learned these things.

I completed the program, to all appearances being successful. I became employed by Teen Challenge New England and New Jersey as a custom software developer and data analyst. God restored the relationship with my daughter and I was able to get to know her again.

I was in a good place, with good people and at a good church. I was enjoying life. I was looking forward to learning what seemed to be the next big lesson—finding romance.

That didn't go well.

She was beautiful. And deadly.

Within five weeks I had left my job, left my church, lost the girl, and fallen into relapse. For the first couple of months I convinced myself I had it together. But there was that gnawing, nagging emptiness. That emptiness that I could fill in one of three ways; with a bottle, with a girl, or with God.

I tried with a girl. But that didn't work.

I went back to the bottle. But the emptiness just got worse.

And worse.

And worse.

And then I came to on April 2, 2009—shaking, sick, looking at the bedside where several empty bottles lay from a weekend bender. One wasn't empty. I faced the choice: Do I take a shot and start to feel better in the short term, or do I suffer through this and get better in the long term?

As I considered the question it was as if the answer came to me as a sledgehammer strike from God. The short-term answer was a quick road to death.

So I suffered.

Two days later I returned to 20 Clifton. I knew I had to return. I wanted to return. But right now? I remember Oscar's words to me that morning: "Henry, you won't survive two weeks. If I had my way I'd have you coming in today."

I hemmed and hawed and recognized what I was doing. The same crap. The same self-deception. Oscar was right—I wasn't going to survive two weeks and I needed to come in that day.

So I did… and that night I had the best night's sleep I'd had in months.

Over the next seven months I began to face who I was and what I had become. I began to let go of anger. I began to look for God for nobody's sake but my own. I began to feel God in a way I never had before. I began to see where I had failed to listen to God's direction. I became enamored of the adventure he had in store for me, knowing full well that the some of the greatest adventures can really suck when you're going through them.

"Happiness is Satan's counterfeit for joy." Reverend Steve Warner once said in a sermon. The apostle James said to "Consider it pure joy, my brothers and sisters, whenever you face trials of many kinds, because you know that the testing of your faith produces perseverance. Let perseverance finish its work so that you may be mature and complete, not lacking anything." The apostle Paul said that he had "learned to be content whatever the circumstances. I know what it is to be in need and I know what it is to have plenty. I have learned the secret of being content in any and every situation, whether well fed or hungry, whether living in plenty or in want."

I came to grips with pain—embracing it not for its own sake, but because I knew that this pain was part of my healing process. I knew that a badly set bone had to be re-broken in order for it to be reset properly. I knew that a festering wound had to be lanced, debrided, and cleaned in order to keep the infection from spreading. All this involved pain, and some of it

severe.

Yet there was *such* joy as I went through this process! I regained friends, made new friends, and found purpose. I committed to doing what God called me to do. And in spite of my fears and feelings, I agreed with God that I would do this:

I would go to California.

It had begun as a joke in my first time through the program. Oscar was from California. A fellow resident I worked with was from California. Both were graduates of the Teen Challenge Ministry Institute. And when this fellow resident lamented in his dislike of Massachusetts, I gloated. I laughed that he had cursed himself to five years in the state.

And then God tapped me on the shoulder.

"Oh, Henry," it seemed like he said in a singsong voice. "You have a fundamental objection to California, don't you?" I thought it was a joke. I refused the call. And I paid the price. When I returned after the relapse I agreed with God that, should he still want me to go, I would go.

God confirmed it in multiple ways.

On June 6, 2013, I departed for South Gate, California, a small city in Los Angeles County, which is home to the Teen Challenge Ministry Institute. I had never before been to California. And it was a shock.

Thank God, though, that Teen Challenge shares a certain feel no matter the location. It didn't matter that I was

48

on the other side of the country from the place I called home. The people here were still Teen Challenge people. They acted in a Teen Challenge fashion. There was a superficial social difference, to be sure. And it was interesting.

If you've ever been to southern California, and especially Los Angeles, you *know* it's a different world. And not merely in the social norms, but in the way the place *works.* I found myself on several Saturday nights walking the streets of downtown Los Angeles—specifically Skid Row. Look it up on Google Maps. Sixth and Maple. Zoom out a little bit—it's actually labeled "Skid Row." After dark the sidewalks turn into their own type of city. Tarps, cardboard boxes, sometimes tents. People who are so far gone they don't know how gone they are. People who landed there looking for a better life. People who landed there because they had nowhere else to live. All deeply hurting. All in need of Jesus. And God opened my heart.

I found myself on several Monday afternoons going to an invalid house. Here the residents were for the most part unable to converse in a way I understood. Here communication happened through a touch, through a smile, through music. There was no Bible study here—*we* were the Bible that these people saw. It was foreign to me. But slowly I began to feel the connection. And God opened my heart.

I found myself walking through towns whose names

49

I couldn't remember, knocking on doors in the hopes of garnering help for Teen Challenge. It seemed that very few people wanted to help. Yet with each door, whether the answer was yes or no, I always thanked the person for their time. And God opened my heart.

In California I learned a strength that I had never before known. I learned the meaning of the phrase "don't trip, it's all good"—a phrase that carried within it the Pauline contentment I so desperately needed to have. In the Pauline contentment I began to truly understand the Jamesian joy. The joy of God transcended mere happiness and became something of its own. It became something I could rest my heart on. And when troubled, when in pain, it became something I could seek out in order to find solace.

Then, on June 9, 2014, I began again in Tallahassee, Florida. I learned the unfortunate lesson of what burnout looks like. I spent a year simply recovering the basis of what brings me joy. With God I sifted through my past, seeking out the pure things. I took to cycling—something that brought me freedom as a child. As an adult it brought me a similar sense of freedom.

After three years in Tallahassee I returned to Massachusetts.

And I had ***come home***.

It was truly amazing. The roads were *right.* The houses were *right.* The way people acted was *right.* The grocery stores were *right.* Everything within me screamed that I had come home.

I had *never before* felt this so strongly.

With merely a nudge and a hint, God brought me back to work at Teen Challenge New England and New Jersey. My job put me back in touch with several old friends. I began making new friends. I enjoyed the challenge of the work put before me as I learned yet another new craft. I became proficient in visual storytelling. I learned how to set up an online video broadcast. I was fulfilled with what I was doing.

I returned to the Vineyard in Kingston. There my friend Paul, who had led the small group I had been a part of before my relapse, let me know that their group would be planting a church in Bridgewater. I joined in with the group knowing God to be behind it.

I was filled with joy and blessed by God with great happiness. I learned more of how to let happiness rest gently in my hand, allowing it to come and go as it would. Happiness is temporary. Joy is from God.

And in the middle of this, God put a wonderful woman in my life.

Her name was Michelle.

I hadn't been looking for her. I hadn't been looking

for *anyone*, for that matter. God started opening my heart, however—especially when I discovered that she was my kind of crazy. As we talked I began walking through the different things I wanted God to provide in the wife he had for me. *And she checked off all the boxes.*

But she was a cancer patient.

Stage IV breast cancer has a way of coming back to kill you. She was stable, but she still had to use an oral treatment regimen. I had to come to terms with the idea of tying my life to someone who could die on me at any moment. I felt, however, that God was leading me into this. He wanted to teach me more about love.

And teach me He did.

A year after we started talking my dear Michelle passed. We were never married. But through our romance I learned more about myself, and more about God, than I had in times prior. I have God to thank for a year that stands without comparison in my life. I have God to thank for the process that brought me to her. I have God to thank that today, as I write this, I know that *He* will fill *all* the places in my heart.

Though there is sorrow, there is also Joy.

And there will always be Joy.

My God is my source of Joy. And that source can never be taken away. It never will be.

No matter what may come my way.

Chapter 3
God is in the Restoration Business

Steve Allain

It was a sunny summer afternoon and I was out riding my red Schwinn Stingray bicycle, with its shiny sissy bar and banana seat, trying to ride wheelies, which I could never quite seem to get the hang of. I spotted a friend of mine who lived up the street, so I rode over to hang out with him. After a short while we stopped to rest and he asked me if I smoked. I said yes which was partly true; I had snuck a cigarette from my parents a few times. We rode our bikes down to the end of the street to a spot where there was a very large rock. We hid behind it and then he pulled out a strange looking cigarette that was hand rolled. He then asked me if I got high, and again I said yes, which this time was a lie. I had never even seen a joint before. We smoked it and though I do not recall getting high, this would be the beginning of my pursuit of altering my state of mind.

Changed Lives

My parents had always allowed us a drink on special occasions. It was their attempt at teaching us to drink socially and responsibly. I am sure they meant well but for me it backfired and I enjoyed it too much. In my last year of middle school, on New Year's Eve, my parents had a party and my sister and I were each given a whole bottle of Cold Duck. My sister didn't want hers, so she gave it to me. I drank both bottles that night. That was my first experience getting drunk and I got so drunk that afterwards I was sick for three days. At only 12 years old, my life was already heading in the wrong direction.

Suddenly, I was entering high school and at 13 years old I was insecure and didn't excel at anything. I was not a great athlete, nor did I excel at academics. I was mediocre in everything I did and mostly by choice. It was a tough process meeting other kids, because I was rather shy. I then discovered marijuana. In 1973 it was relatively inexpensive; a $10 bag would last all month and I could stay high all day every day and found I was no longer so self-conscious. I started playing sports, first on the football team and eventually migrating over to the track team because I found out I was really good at the high jump. I was clearing 5' 10" my junior year and 6' my senior year. This was often enough to place 1st or 2nd at track meets, sometimes 3rd on a bad day.

Smoking marijuana everyday made me very lazy and lethargic when it came to schoolwork. I managed to graduate, but I never had any interest in what was being taught. After I graduated high school, I had no desire to go to college, so I got a job with the city. I was a groundskeeper in a cemetery (talk about a dead-end job) and I was drinking every night and going out to bars. One night in August of 1976, I went to a house party where I proceeded to get mind-numbing drunk. As I was driving home I ended up hitting a parked car. The police were called and I was arrested. I was only 17 years old and my blood alcohol level was way over the legal limit. The next day I went to court and the judge suspended my driver's license indefinitely. I was already doing a pretty good job of messing up my life. Since I lived close to the cemetery I could walk to work but without the ability to drive a car, I was severely limited from living the way I had been. I had to depend on friends for rides if I wanted to go out or walk to the bars that were close enough to my parents' house.

One fall day while I was out in the cold cutting grass and digging holes for coffins, I realized that I had to make a change. Three weeks after my 18th birthday I went to see an Air Force military recruiter and eleven days later I was headed to Wichita Falls, Texas for Air Force basic training boot camp. I was able to choose a job when I joined, and I chose computer operator. I made it through basic training and headed to San Antonio, Texas to start my occupational training. After completing occupational training, I started my stint in the Air Force and was assigned to a base in the middle of the Atlantic

Changed Lives

Ocean at Lajes Field on Terceira Island in Azores, Portugal. Since I was being stationed overseas, it was required that I have a valid US driver's license, so I went back to the court with a letter from the U.S. Government stating that they had to release the suspension on my driver's license. Nine months after my license was suspended indefinitely, I walked out of the courtroom with an active driver's license once again. There was not much to do on a small island for an 18-year-old, so I did what I knew best; went to the bars. I also became pretty good at shooting pool.

My Air Force career was uneventful, and I decided to not re-enlist when my time was up. I was looking forward to getting back to civilian life and starting my career working with computers. Now back in Massachusetts I moved in with my parents who were gracious enough to let me live there for a while until I could get a job. My relationship with them hadn't been that good mainly because of my rebellious attitude. However, the military had changed me and I learned how to take orders and submit to authority. I started building a good relationship with my father with meaningful conversations, which had never really happened before. Joining the Air Force had also given him something to be proud of me for.

My relationship with my father was still evolving when a few months later my mother woke me up at 2:30 in the morning saying we had to go to the hospital right away. My father was taken away in an ambulance. I remember that night so well. We were all sitting and waiting for word from the doctor. My mother hadn't told us that my father had a heart attack because she didn't want to worry us. After about a half hour the doctor walked into the room. The look on the doctor's face was grim and he said, "I am sorry, but we did everything we could." I don't remember much after that except that my head fell back on the chair and I was in total disbelief. How could this be? My father was never sick. He never missed a day of work and suddenly out of nowhere he was dead. I could not wrap my mind around his death. We were just starting to get along. My mother took it the hardest of all as my father was everything to her.

The next year started a slow and steady downward spiral. I was still drinking regularly when I was introduced to cocaine by a co-worker. At first, I only used it occasionally, but it didn't take long before it became a full-fledged addiction that would steer the direction of my life for the next few years. My family grew tired of this and soon wanted nothing to do with me. Before I knew it, I was an addict and I couldn't be trusted. My mother told my two younger brothers and me that I was no longer welcome to live in their home. I spent about a year going from place to place trying to get a grasp on what was happening to me. My family disowned me, I was virtually homeless, and I saw no hope in sight. I thought that a geographical change would benefit me and help me overcome my addiction. I had a friend in Ft. Lauderdale, Florida who told me that I could come down and stay with him for a while. I bought a plane ticket, flew to Florida and attempted to start over. I never intended to stop drinking or smoking marijuana I just wanted to stop using cocaine. I did well for a while and started working as a plumber's apprentice. It wasn't long before someone at the job site offered me a little afternoon bump from his stash. This was the early 80's and cocaine had started coming into this country like a flood, quite a bit of it through Florida. The supply was plentiful, pure, and cheap. Soon a new form of cocaine was introduced to the streets nicknamed "crack" because of the sound it made when you smoked it. I started to use it since the powder form wasn't available on the streets. This took my addiction to new levels and took me to a place of total despair.

Like most people who find themselves a slave to a substance, the addiction took over my life. My relationship with my family in Massachusetts dissolved completely. They couldn't understand why I couldn't just stop. My mother would say, "If you love me you would stop using." I was on my own with no family, no friends, and in a place that I didn't know. I survived by what I thought was wit and luck, but I was wrong. Eventually I found out that the only reason I survived was because of God. I was moving from place to place and at times slept by the intracoastal river in a sleeping bag on the ground. Another place I would stay when I saved up enough money was a weekly rental studio apartment. It was the now summer 1985 and I had been doing well for a couple of months, meaning I was able to pay rent and stay in one place. The young manager at the apartment complex always had a good word to say and lived in a way that I could tell there was something different about him. He was happy, but it was more than that, though I couldn't quite put my finger on it. He lived in the manager's apartment there and drove an old Chevy Impala. When I saw him around, he seemed to always carry a big black book with him. I found out it was a Bible and that he was going to seminary studying to be a pastor. My only experience with God, Jesus, or religion was that as a boy I went to a Catholic church with my mother now and then. I remember thinking that I wanted whatever he had. Walking past his car one day I saw a bumper sticker that said, "Lake Worth Baptist Church." I had a feeling that what he had he found there.

The next Sunday I went to that church. It seemed like the pastor was speaking directly to me. At the end of his message he asked if there was anybody that wanted a new start, their sins forgiven, their slate wiped clean, and give their life to Jesus. Sitting there in the back unshaven, in jeans that were full of holes and not real clean, I wanted to go up and get a new start. Then a voice said if you go up front everyone in here will know you're a sinner. The pastor asked again, and I said to myself "you *are* a sinner." So I got out of my seat and walked to the front. The very next Sunday I was baptized as a public profession of my faith and my journey as a Christian

61

began!

An amazing thing had happened to me! I was born again into a new life and into the family of God. I became involved in the church and was going to every service that the church had as well as the singles Bible study. I volunteered to do the van pickups on Sunday morning for the elderly and for families that didn't have a ride to church. I started working with the Royal Rangers, which is the church's version of Boy Scouts. Everything was going so well, I got a new job as a landscaper, started working full-time, and was able to rent a full apartment rather than a studio with a shared bathroom like before. I had a lot to learn about my new life, about God, and the church. My desire to get high or drink had disappeared; all I wanted to do was serve God.

The singles Tuesday night Bible study was where I started to gain knowledge about God, I was soaking it all in. We digested, dissected, and discussed the Word of God. I was building good godly relationships with people I considered more than friends I considered them family. Life had taken a turn for the good and I was on top of the mountain. I came home from work one day and the singles Bible study leader was waiting for me at the door of my apartment. Completely unexpectedly, this married father of a teenage daughter told me that he was falling in love with me! This situation caught me off guard and I was not sure how to handle it. Because I did not know anyone I could talk to about it, I stopped going to the singles Bible study and eventually stopped going to church. Soon I began hanging out at bars again, which led back to using drugs and soon I lost my job and my apartment. I was right back to life as it was before Jesus.

I decided to stay at a rescue mission instead of sleeping on the streets. While there, I became friends with a man who was headed to Sacramento, California. I asked him if I could join him on his trip and within three weeks we were on our way. Things were looking up again and we had a place to stay at a church and after working a bit doing whatever I could for minimum wage, I was offered a job as a teamster loading and unloading trucks at a major trucking freight line. This lasted for about a year but it wasn't long before I was drinking and using drugs again, but this time it didn't last long. I checked myself into a long-term residential Christian rehabilitation program.

As soon as I entered the program I felt at home. I was more like training for ministry than a program. There was an overwhelming sense of a family atmosphere and I knew that this was where I wanted to be. The pastor was a gifted man and was also a creative architect before he entered ministry. He wrote a drama that depicted his family life, riddled by the effects of gangs and drugs. The many youth in our church family were sold out for Jesus and we practiced the drama many times a week before taking it to the steps of the state capitol in Sacramento. The well-written play and actors were convincing. Most of them came from the life of gangs and drugs themselves and were now living lives that glorified God.

We travelled the west coast with the drama in the hopes that lives would be changed and people would come to Christ and be born again by the message of hope and love of Christ that was demonstrated in the play. As news spread we started to get bookings in Nevada, Colorado, Texas, and Hawaii. Then in 1996 we were asked to take the drama out of the country to South America. The two places we went were Bogota, Columbia and Caracas, Venezuela. Talk about a culture shock, that trip was life transforming. There was so much pain and desperation you could feel it in the air. It is still a vivid picture in my mind of people sitting on the side of the road dressed in dirty rags with fingernails two to three inches long and their hands out begging for change. A few pennies were all they needed because cocaine was only 15 cents a gram. No food per se, but plenty of drugs.

During my 18-year stay in California, I would fly back to visit my family as much as possible, which was not often. They still didn't trust me and I could not blame them. They had no idea that I was undergoing a transformation. I was born again and God was sanctifying me. They only knew the person that I was and they had been too hurt to allow that again. However, during one of those trips I was invited to a family cookout. This was a big deal to me; it felt like I was starting to be forgiven. While there I spoke for quite a while to a woman who was a friend of the family and I remember walking away from the conversation asking God, "How come *I* can't meet a woman like that?"

I was single and had dedicated my life to serving God wherever He wanted me to go. We travelled around with the drama for about six years and then things started to dissolve as the cast grew older and moved onto college or work. The leadership's vision also turned to other directions and the church started to lose focus. The pastor wouldn't submit to the leadership over him and was told he could no longer be a part of the denomination. Many of us agreed with the leadership and didn't follow the pastor to his new denomination he then served under. This was hard to take because this was my family and all I knew. I was alone again and everything changed. My relationship with God had grown distant over the last few years due to so much "ministry." I had lost touch with the God I was serving. There was no longer anyone I was accountable to, no leadership in my life, and no church family to be part of anymore. I was confused and without direction again and before I knew it, I was using cocaine. I couldn't believe it. How was it possible that I was using again after so many years of sobriety? Since I was not the same person I was before, I quickly found another Christian program staffed by some friends of mine that I knew in the former ministry. This program was Teen Challenge. I entered Teen Challenge in Sacramento, California and graduated the program 12 months later.

I chose to stay on and work as an intern there for about three months and then started to get a desire to move back to the east coast. I didn't have any money saved and was not sure how I would go about this. I had a strong desire to see if there was any way that I could restore some type of relationship with my mother, sister, and brothers. I started to look online for any Teen Challenge programs in Southeastern Massachusetts with the hopes that they would have some sort of reentry program that they would let me transfer over to. I came across the Teen Challenge New England and New Jersey's website and sent an email to the director. A few days later I received an email back from Dr. Rodney Hart. I had only been in Teen Challenge for a little over a year but in that short time I had heard about Dr. Hart as he was well known throughout the ministry. In the email he stated that they didn't have a reentry program, but he said there was probably a spot for someone like me in the ministry of Teen Challenge New England and New Jersey. He gave me his personal cell phone number and said if I was interested to give him a call, so I did.

The call to Dr. Hart was promising, but since he had never met me he wanted to do an interview first. Me being on the west coast and him being on the east coast made this a bit challenging, but God is still God and it just so happened that a graduate of Teen Challenge Massachusetts (Brockton) was in Davis, California just a few miles away from Sacramento. Dr. Hart gave me his phone number and we set up a meeting.

After the interview I was told that there was a place for me at Teen Challenge New England and New Jersey. I bought a one-way ticket to Boston and stayed a little while in my hometown before entering Teen Challenge Greater Boston as an intern. I worked there for just about 10 years, during which time I helped in the office doing IT and various other office tasks. I was also blessed being a part of the team that went to different churches on Sunday to sing, play music, and to bring a message of hope to the people who had family members with life controlling challenges such as drug and alcohol addiction. This was an amazing time in my life; my job was serving God and His people. Quite often when we went from church to church on Sunday I would be asked to preach, which was quite an honor and so then I decided to further my education and knowledge by going to Bible College. I applied to Gordon Conwell Theological Seminary and was accepted into the Master of Arts program even though I had never gone to college. This was a probationary enrollment and was contingent upon doing well in the first seven courses. I finished the seven courses with a GPA high enough to continue on with the master's program and received a diploma in Theological Studies.

Since the main reason that I wanted to move back to the east coast was a desperate attempt to reconcile with my family, I thought that if they saw me every day or at least occasionally, they would see that I had changed and would eventually forgive me. That is not possible now for some and does not look promising for the rest who are still alive. When I got back to the east coast I didn't know where or how to get in touch with my siblings because I didn't know their addresses and my mother would not tell me. So even though I was not sure how anyone felt about me; I thought they all hated me. Through social media I reached out to a couple of people to find out where my brothers and sister lived. I took a chance to see if I would get a favorable response. I didn't say that I was back on the east coast, I just said hi. I afraid of being rejected and didn't get my hopes up. They both said hi back and I left it there not knowing what to say or do next. One of them was Pam, the woman I mentioned earlier that I asked God why I couldn't meet someone like her.

A few months went by and I received a message from Pam asking me if I knew someone that could help her son, she knew I was involved in a ministry that helped people with addiction issues. I responded that I was on the east coast and that I could indeed help and would be glad to. My phone rang and it was Pam. She told me that her son was homeless and having problems. He was involved in a drug deal gone bad and was stuck at a store. It just so happened that I was ten minute drive from that store, even though I lived nowhere near there. I got his phone number, called him, and asked him if he needed a ride. I picked him up and brought him to the Teen Challenge Massachusetts (Brockton) center and then back to where he was living at the time. He eventually went into the Teen Challenge program, and is doing very well to this day. During the time of his stay at Teen Challenge, I occasionally started hanging out with his mother. To make a long story short on February 2, 2012 I asked Pam to marry me and she said yes. God's answer to my prayer about finding a woman like her was answered in the most direct way possible, after 18 years! After we were married, I moved into Pam's was rented house and I continued working at Teen Challenge Greater Boston.

Two years later we decided to buy a house. God provided a nice little fixer-upper with a reasonable mortgage. I also realized that it was time to move on from Teen Challenge, after over 10 years of service. I sent out one resume. Within five days I received a response and was invited to an interview, and three days I was offered the position.

I have lived on two different continents, in three different countries, eight different states, and about 20 different cities. The house we bought is less than a mile away from the one I was born and raised in. God truly is in the business of restoration. He has kept me and continues to bless me beyond what I deserve. I am still involved in ministry although not vocationally, as before. He has healed my mind, body, and soul. Because of Him I live. He has given me a job close to home, a wife who loves Jesus and is my best friend, and a house that we can call home. God has truly given me more than I could have ever imagined. My desire in life is to continue to serve Him and allow Him to direct my steps.

Chapter 4
Chased to God

Aaron Burtsell

My name is Aaron Burtsell, and I'm 53 years old. Born and raised in Nashua, NH, I considered my family to be normal for the most part. I grew up in the low-income housing projects of Nashua, surrounded by people living similar lives. My mother took care of the house, showed us love and affection, disciplined us, and was everything someone could ask for in a mother. My father, on the other hand, was a Korean War veteran and was greatly affected by that experience. In our house, he served as nothing more than a provider and just another person living in the house. He worked hard to make sure all the bills were paid, the family was fed, and there were clothes on our backs, but that was all he did. He didn't know how to express love or compassion and I never saw any emotion or received and affection from him. Most of the time, his facial expression was emotionless. I gave up on trying to receive affection from him. Though I wanted it, I just got used to the feeling of living without it. Looking back on it today, there was really no father figure in my life growing up.

I had five brothers and one sister, and all my brothers were either alcoholics or drug addicts. As a result, I saw that kind of lifestyle as something unavoidable and just a normal part of life for people from the projects in Nashua and so I followed suit. I was in special needs classes from 5th grade all the way through high school due to a learning disability. Learning disabilities were looked at as more of a disease rather than a handicap, so I was separated from everybody. This made life extremely difficult for me. I became frustrated with the limitations that came along with being unable to learn as efficiently as others, and I saw how the other kids in my classes were treated because of their disabilities. I felt it necessary to fight anybody and everybody who thought I was weak because of it. Having older brothers, I spent a lot of time hanging out with kids much older and more experienced than I was, and this introduced me to substances at a much younger age.

The neighborhood I lived in was always chaotic. It seemed as if there was always something going on whether it be drinking, smoking, fighting, or general trouble. I started smoking cigarettes when I was nine years old. To me, it wasn't some forbidden or foreign thing, it was normal. Cigarettes led to alcohol, alcohol led to marijuana, and by the age of twelve I was heavily into using LSD. I was just going with the flow. If it was there, I was doing it, regardless of what it was. Being the second youngest of all my brothers, and the family history of drugs and alcohol, as I said earlier it was kind of like I was just following in their footsteps. The life of addiction was ready and waiting to take hold of me.

I made a strong effort to lead a normal life. The Boys Club in Nashua was something that set me up to have a great future. I was heavily involved there, partly because there wasn't a whole lot going on at home, but I also felt a sense of purpose and comradery there. Over the course of four years, the swim team, floor hockey, and boxing gave me a sense of companionship and accomplishment I'd been missing in my life. My mentor, Steve, really took me under his wing, tried to guide me in right and wrong almost like a father-figure, but the pull of my environment, one I'd spent much more time in than the Boys Club, was just too strong.

God was never spoken of in my house, so I had no understanding of anything that had to do with religion, until I met Billy. When I was thirteen years old, I had a next-door neighbor, Billy, who I thought was a complete nutjob. I couldn't understand how someone could be so happy all the time. We used to call him the "Jesus Freak" because that's all he ever talked about. My friends and I truly made a valiant effort at making this guy's life a living nightmare. We harassed him, did figure eights with cars on his lawn, and blew the back door off his house several times with M80 fireworks. The thing I remember most about him, however, was that he never seemed to get frustrated or angry with us, he just kept trying to tell us about this Jesus person. After a relentless year of trying to tell me about Christ, I reluctantly agreed to go to a service with him out of sheer curiosity.

I had no idea what I was getting into. The church he brought me to was ultra-Pentecostal. There were people cheering and praying all around me. However, I felt something pulling in my heart to walk up to the altar, like a faint tug trying to bring me towards a better life. As I was up there, the pastor of the church laid hands on me and I gave my life to Christ right there and then. It was a sensation I had never felt before. Electricity slowly surged throughout my body, and at that very moment in time I was overwhelmed with tremendous peace. I knew my life was going to be different, I just didn't know when.

I liked the feeling I received from letting Christ into my life. I went to church, men's meetings, and anything else that revolved around God for about seven months. Despite my hunger for the Lord, I was still susceptible to sin, and I didn't know how to overcome that. At 14, we would go out in the woods three or four times a week and drink. We would have bonfires, get older kids to buy as alcohol; it was just the thing to do. I could have never foreseen this becoming a problem, but it slowly developed into a drinking problem as I got older. Again, I succumbed to the environment around me, but this time there was no Boy's Club, no Pentecostal Church service that was going to keep me back, and the next 20 years of my life were nothing like I had drawn up in my head. It's funny, even though I walked away from the Lord, I still knew, that I knew, He was still with me. His presence never left my life no matter what way I was living.

I stopped going to church with Billy and continued with my "normal" life through high school. After walking away from the Boy's Club and church, there was nobody I could look up to, no role model that was there to guide me through life. I just went with the crowd. I was 16 when I first started using cocaine. Funny enough, none of it really did anything special for me, it was just what everybody was doing. I began selling drugs in high school which allowed me to not work and continue to use the way I wanted to use. I dropped out of high school in 11th grade to pursue my career as a drug dealer and started shooting cocaine shortly after dropping out. By 19 years old I was first arrested for possession and sales trying to support my habit. I was sentenced to one to three years in New Hampshire state prison.

Prison was tough. Not tough as in violence or anything like that, but it was just a ticking clock, and I was wasting

75

away in there. I was confined to close quarters and knew I couldn't leave until my time was up. Every movement I made was under the direction of the guards and I truly lost all sense of freedom. There was nothing profitable for me, nothing to help me. They didn't have the programs they have today to try to rehabilitate inmates. I swore I'd never go back.

I did a lot of drugs in prison, so my efforts to never go back were completely obliterated by substances. I never went to church, Bible study, nothing constructive. I never sought the Lord, and in return never felt His presence. I didn't learn anything except how to continue being a criminal. The day I got out of prison, I immediately started drinking and pretty much picked up from where I left off. I soon started using drugs again, couldn't hold a job, and went back to prison on a parole violation to finish the rest of my three years. The first thing I did when I got out was get a half gallon of vodka. I put no effort into trying to walk the straight line.

About a year after my release from prison, I was arrested again for drug possession with intent to distribute. By this time, I couldn't support my drug habit by working a regular job so selling drugs was my only option. If it weren't for the drugs, I would have never seen the inside of a prison, but I just couldn't escape the grip they had on me and truly saw no way out. In the midst of having to bounce people out of my house one night, a man pulled a gun out and stuck the barrel

76

straight into my forehead. Despite the feeling of cold steel on my head, I had a warm sense of relief as I begged him to pull the trigger. I was ready to die; I just didn't care anymore.

The man never pulled the trigger that evening, but I was raided shortly thereafter. The door was kicked down, the police threw in a couple flashbang grenades, and off to prison I went again. It seemed like God was trying many different ways to get my attention while sparing my life. I was sentenced to 2½ to 7 years in prison. I said I'd never go back, but there I was again, using drugs, and still far away from the Lord. I just accepted the fact that this was how my life was going to continue to be. Released on parole and living in a halfway house, I started going to New Beginnings Church after meeting Pastor Sonny Dean while I was in prison. I started getting into the Word of God at that point, but had difficulty applying it to my life since I was still battling drugs and alcohol. There I also met the founder of Teen Challenge New Hampshire, Pastor Steve Gadomski, and that man chased me down for the next decade of my life.

At the age of 27, my girlfriend at the time became pregnant with my daughter, Cheyenne. I didn't really want any extra responsibility, I mean, how could I be responsible for someone else when I couldn't even be responsible for myself? So, I moved to Florida, abandoning my girlfriend during her pregnancy. I came back right after my daughter was born, tried to work our relationship out, but that ended up being a total disaster. When Cheyenne was about a year old, I went back to prison, and during my time there, Cheyenne's mother lost custody of her and my daughter was placed in foster care. I'm not really sure where her mother went. While I was in prison, there were certain things I needed to do in order to obtain custody of Cheyenne when I got out, so I began taking steps in the right direction. I was released from prison, and after a few years of state-supervised visits I was awarded custody. Interacting with my daughter for the first time was rough. I didn't know how to be a father, I had been in and out of prison my whole life, and her mother was nowhere to be found.

I was doing well for a while. I had an apartment, a job working for a cable company in Manchester, New Hampshire, and my mother was helping me out with daycare and raising Cheyenne. I was able to drink socially, enjoy time with friends, and live a normal life. I did pretty well for almost three years. One random weekend at a party I met a girl and I decided to get high with her. I immediately abandoned everything for drugs again. I knew I was going to keep using and there was no way I was going to stop. Out of desperation I packed up my daughter's belongings, put her on the stoop of my mother's house, banged on the door, and left her there on the front steps of her grandmother's house. Then off I went, for two more years.

At this point in my life, I felt like there was no turning back. I was using more than I ever had and was completely out of control. Once again, I was arrested for possession with intent to distribute and sentenced to another seven years in prison. I suppose at this point I should have realized there was no controlling my drug use. However, the devil had a funny way of allowing me to forget all the trouble drugs and alcohol brought me. Eventually, I was again released on parole and found it difficult to live a life free from drugs and alcohol. I was 36 years old, didn't have a job, didn't have custody of Cheyenne, and was in and out of prison. I felt like there was no hope for me, and the best thing I could do was kill myself and get it over with. I went to a hotel room that night and injected enough cocaine to kill an elephant. I shot it and began sensing the life leaving me. Everything was fading into blackness except for two small white dots in the center of my vision, then suddenly, at the very last minute, before everything became totally dark, I instantaneously felt normal again. The next thing I knew, I found myself outside of my hotel sitting in a snowbank. The Lord told me that from that day on things were going to change.

Two weeks later I was arrested for possession with intent to distribute for the third time. I was now facing 14 to 30 years in prison under the 3-Strike Rule yet confusingly, I felt this confident peace inside of me. While locked-up in Valley

79

Street jail, once again Pastor Steve Gadomski and Pastor Sonny Dean walked into my life. It was there I reconnected with the Lord. I was reading my Bible, praying, engaging the chapel services, and really becoming inspired to focus on my relationship with Christ. I thought about all the chances I'd had to do this over the course of my life, wondering if I was really going to get the chance to give this "Life in Christ" thing a real shot.

I can still remember the day like it was yesterday. Approaching the hour of arraignment, the Lord came into my heart and told me to pack my stuff up because I was never going back to jail. I really didn't know how that was going to be possible. Here I was, a convicted felon, on parole, and arrested again, but I felt deep down inside I'd never see the inside of a jail cell again, and I've never been back since.

I met Pastor Steve roughly ten years ago and I saw him everywhere; in jail, out of jail, random places like alleyways in Nashua. I just couldn't escape the guy. Every time I saw him, he would try to get me to go to Teen Challenge. So, when I walked out of court that day, free to make my own decisions again, I called him and he got me in to Teen Challenge in Brockton, Massachusetts on November 22, 2002.

Teen Challenge is not easy. It was very structured and work oriented. Every day I would get up at 4am to open the kitchen, work all day and night while doing my Learning

Center and going to prayer throughout the day. It was a 24/7 process, but exactly what I needed. Praise the Lord I was baptized in the Spirit four months into the program, because if it wasn't for the strength of Christ through that baptism, I would have never made it. I couldn't understand what I was doing there and why I was doing it. God gave me wisdom, understanding, and knowledge of what I was supposed to do and why I was supposed to do it, and that was to simply serve Him, whatever that looked like. Fortunately, God placed some great people in my life, like Richie Longo, who mentored me. He placed everything in terms of the Bible and the will of God, and that was what allowed me to continue to learn how to live, be productive, and be open to the influence of God of my life. I wouldn't have said it at the time, but looking back on it now I see that it was the most fruitful time of learning how to serve, how to listen to mentors placed in my life, and how to mentor those God entrusted to me.

The curriculum was the hardest thing for me to overcome. I was a slow learner and the kitchen allowed me to avoid the Learning Center at all costs, but in order to graduate I needed to complete it. God proves time and time again He will use the things you least expect to shape and mold you into who He's created you to be. The courses I had to take, specifically Group Studies, made a huge impact in my life. My favorite one was Anger and Personal Rights, and I still talk about it to this day. When I became angry, nothing good came from it, and it took me about a year with God working on me repeatedly in this area to make progress. This group study helped me greatly to get ahold of my anger, which was a huge catalyst for my drug use. Because I was so driven by my emotions, I was no good to anybody when I was angry, and this book taught me how to manage my emotions constructively. It was life-changing.

I graduated from Brockton in 2004 and the 14-30 years in prison I was facing disappeared. God is truly a miracle worker. I felt Him calling me to stay with Teen Challenge as I still had a lot to learn and found a desire to serve those in the same place as I once was. I served as the Kitchen Coordinator there until my mother was unable to care for Cheyenne and I needed to become the father God created me to be. Pastor Steve had started Teen Challenge New Hampshire a few years prior and offered for me to come work as their Kitchen Coordinator in 2005, so I could begin the restoration process with my daughter. It was all new to me. I was living in the apartment at New Beginnings Church establishing a stable environment for Cheyenne, and when she was 10 years old, I obtained custody of her. I will always be indebted to Teen Challenge for helping me get her back, and even more so to Noreen Gadomski for helping me to raise a 10-year-old girl.

Life with Christ doesn't mean there won't be struggles.

After reuniting with my longtime friend and finding the love of my life, Kim, we were married on July 1, 2013. Kim was not without struggles of her own. She was an amazing artist, a wonderful woman, and my best friend, but she also struggled with the same demons I did. We went through several years of her being clean and using on and off, in and out of jail on probation violations, and in and out of detoxes. Through it all, I remained faithful to Christ and sobriety, but it was one of the most difficult times of my life. After spending a year in jail on another violation, Kim was released to a women's shelter where she overdosed and died. I was disappointed and angry with her, but it was very short because the will of God is bigger than my questions. It was a very difficult time for me, but I had the Lord to lean on. I don't know what I would've done if not for Christ. I didn't miss a single day of work.

Overall, I could have never dreamed of the life I have today. Cheyenne grew up in the Teen Challenge family. She graduated high school and served six years in the military. She is now going back to college and our relationship has been amazing since I became a real father to her. I am now the Program Supervisor, the Work Crew Supervisor, and run our Teen Challenge landscaping company. I obtained my driver's license at the age of 38 and my first bank account at the age of 40. I live in my own apartment and have my own car (and have never been late on a payment)! I've been blessed enough to

83

own a beautiful Harley Davidson motorcycle, something I've wanted for as long as I can remember. God has far exceeded any and all my expectations.

Aside from the work, the ministry, relationships, love, loss, blessings, trials, and the everyday business of life, the greatest thing I've received is the peace and freedom only Christ can give. I no longer crave any substances because He set me free. I no longer yearn for fulfillment in relationships, work, or anything else the world offers. The greatest lesson I've learned through it all is to always stay the course and never give up, because God is faithful. He changed my life and He can change yours too!

Chapter 5
Jesus Boot Camp

Sheila Flanders [Clark]

My life began in Clinton, Connecticut with my parents, my older brother, Matthew and my younger brother, Paul. When I was four, we moved to Castile, New York where my parents attended Elohim Baptist Bible Institute for three years. While living there, I was sexually abused by a neighbor on several occasions and his brother also assaulted our babysitter while she was watching us. This affected my life negatively for many years and I never told anyone, until one day in 1989 when I entered a counseling group. I always felt very self-conscious and so I looked for acceptance in unhealthy ways to hide the pain. As a teenager, I was an awful, rebellious child that was out of control. I tried to be the class clown.

My dad has always been there for me without being judgmental. He visited me many times while I went from treatment center to treatment center. My mom struggled with

PTSD from abuse she suffered as a child. We had some rough times and she was a strict disciplinarian but when I reached adulthood we were able to make amends with each other. To this day our relationship remains close and she is there for me. She kept God's promise, found in Proverbs 22:26, close to her heart until it came to fruition, "Start children off on the way they should go, and even when they are old they will not turn from it." I now honor my mother and father and show them the utmost respect.

In 1975, after my parents graduated Bible school, we moved to Bridgeport, Connecticut where my father was hired as an interim pastor. It was one of the darkest times of our lives. My brother Matthew was bullied and abused and he turned to drugs. At only 11 years, I soon followed and began using drugs and alcohol too. At times, I would venture into the scariest housing projects in Bridgeport. Looking back, I now know the Lord kept me alive through every dangerous moment. God always had a plan.

Living in Bridgeport, I witnessed so much violence. I saw and heard things as a child which made me turn to the streets and act tough. In third grade I saw a woman get stabbed in the neck. There were arson fires right behind our house that I would watch out my window. I would go to bed each night wondering if the police were ever going to find the man who raped and killed two little sisters, ages three and five, right in my own neighborhood. As young as I was, I heard he hid them inside a refrigerator.

My life progressed into more frequently abusing even harder drugs. My parents moved us to Florida and then divorced only a few years later. At 17, I left and returned to Bridgeport. By the time I was 19, I weighed only 103lbs and was close to death as a result of using crack. I worked night and day to get drugs. In the hospital after an overdose, a nurse asked me, "Where are your parents?" I said, "Florida, and I am on my own." She said to me, "Do you think you're doing a good job?" I put my head down and finally realized that I was dying and I needed help. I went home and slept for 24 hours straight. When I woke up, I was able to admit it and say out loud "I am an addict." But now what? I called my mom, a friend, and I told my roommate. He had a friend who was able to get me into Bridgeport Mental Health Center that night. I needed to detox and I already had an enlarged liver. After 28 days, I was warned to get out of Bridgeport. They suggested the Murphy Center in Willimantic, Connecticut. I had to buy a map, not knowing where it was, but I went!

I was able to put together two years sober but I was living in sexual immorality and other sin. I spent the next 17 years in and out of sobriety. I went through about 20 different inpatient and outpatient programs and was put on medication with many different diagnoses. At 25, I had a daughter who

I loved very much but still could not stay sober. By this time, most of the people in my life had given up on me and thought I would die an addict.

It may sound strange, but even throughout this time, I always loved the Lord and knew the truth! I knew that there was a better way to live and that God wanted my obedience, but I was in so very deep. I would attend church because I knew that I didn't need to be well to go there. There were short periods of trying to get sober and doing some good in this world. I always had a heart for the homeless and the lost. There were times where I would actually ruin my high and the high of others because I would feel so guilty and horrible for the way I was living. Whenever I heard the song, Will You Love Jesus More?, I would cry so hard. I didn't know how to love Jesus more than drugs, but I would beg Him to help me. I hated hurting everyone around me, but I just couldn't stop! Crack cocaine controlled me from the first moment I smoked it that day in 1987. It would take 21 years before I allowed God to finally take it away. Now it no longer calls me! Thank you, God!

For the most part of my life I was a functioning addict and workaholic. Several of my jobs would let me go to treatment and then come back. I actually held one job for nine years, though I was living a double life. There were also some very low moments that I was unable to hide. I burned more and more bridges as I continued to live wrong. Yet, somehow I still would strive to be the person that I know God meant for me to be. I always felt called to the medical field. I yearned to help my addict friends and others, but I was still in slavery to my own sin. Every now and then when I was able to give up the substances, I would still stay living in other sin. Still, I knew that God wanted me to help people and I continually prayed for Him to make me sober. I really wanted Him to use me, but I loved getting high more. For a very long time, I remained filled with so much bitterness, unforgiveness, and self-hatred.

The trauma, abuse, and neglect I had experienced for most of my life continued; my brother committed suicide (his body was unidentifiable), both of my parents attempted suicide, and many of my friends were dead from drugs or from suicide. Too many times, I dealt with the aftermath of sudden deaths and I had to clean out apartments or make phone calls to notify loved ones. Not surprisingly, all of this added up to my diagnosis of PTSD and at times I too contemplated suicide.

I attended Ashford Baptist Church with my mother from 1998 until 2005. That is where I first heard about Teen Challenge. When the choirs came and visited the church, the men or women would share their testimonies. I never wanted to go there because at 15 months, it was way too long! I continued with counseling and was in and out of short-term programs to detox and then try to stay sober.

Changed Lives

In 2008, I was living with a woman named Carolyn, who has disabilities and was wheelchair bound. I was paid to take care of her. One night, because of my addiction, I didn't make it home to care for Carolyn's needs. I called and was honest about being high and so she had to call others for help. The fact that I left her stranded was so hard for me to bear. I reached a point in my addiction were I knew I was going to die if I did not stop and I needed to go to Teen Challenge! I even had a vision on March 5, 2008 of my daughter standing over my graveside and I knew these events were true turning points towards God and away from death! I could not run anymore. The next morning, I sat at Carolyn's bedside and cried saying, "Okay, I will go to Teen Challenge." The two weeks leading up to my day of deliverance was pure hell (I will leave it at that) and the devil tried everything to keep me from turning to the Lord at Teen Challenge!

By the grace of God, I ended up at Teen Challenge Rhode Island. It has been used to change many women's lives, mine included. At the time, there were two homes with four to six women sharing a room. We had chores, prayer time in the chapel, choir practices, work, study hall, fellowship, donation pick-ups, DAT, and canning. Did I also mention work around the center? The days were extremely long and because I was a driver, my hours were extended. Most days started at 6am, but because I wanted to be in control, I was

awake before the staff arrived to wake us. I wanted to be able to use the bathroom quickly and be ready on time! I tried very hard not to get in trouble, although when I did get in some, I understood that it was time alone with God and He always had a message for me. If I attended evening prayer time, my day ended about 11pm. I knew that I must do all God had for me in this program because He clearly showed me that it was my last chance at recovery.

Each evening we received our schedule for the next day telling us where we were going and which staff would be working. I would often get mad because it was such a full schedule and not what "I expected." One particular time, when I had already pressed my choir uniform because I thought I was going on choir ministry, at 10pm the schedule was changed and the staff told me I was to attend one of our home churches instead. I had a bad attitude and I was angry. At church that next day the guest speaker was Pasco Manzo. Although I did not know him well, we would listen to his sermons during chapel sometimes. That morning when he preached, I knew exactly why God had switched the schedule. It was a powerful and inspirational teaching. Everything he was saying was as if the Lord had a special message just for me! Even down to the last details of one of his stories about a young lady from the "Hooker Hotel" in Willimantic, the place I moved to at the age of 19 years old! I was well aware of the place, as most addicts were. I asked if I could speak to him after the service and was allowed to. God let me see that when I surrendered to Him and His plans and purposes, it was for my benefit.

Being in Teen Challenge for two years, two weeks and two days (yes we counted the days) was one of the hardest things I ever did. The Lord showed me that I needed to finish! It was a matter of life or death. For even when the doors were open for me to leave when I completed the program after 18½ months, I knew the Lord wanted me to stay for another six months for the staff apprenticeship, so that He could continue to work in my life. I would be able to show the other ladies in the program that people can change and to teach them what I had learned. I had hope for the first time in my life! I was staying sober and God transformed my mind. God plucked me out of the world for a time and wanted me immersed in His word and the truth! 2 Timothy 3:16-17 says, "All scripture is God-breathed and is useful for teaching, rebuking, correcting and training in righteousness, so that that servant of God may be thoroughly equipped for every good work." God has used me since I graduated and I have never been more fulfilled in my life.

The verse that I have stood upon since Teen Challenge is Jeremiah 33:3, "Call to me, and I will answer you and show you great and mighty things, which you do not know." I know that when things are not good and the enemy is at work and I am confused, I can call out to God Almighty and He will reveal to me the truth. As long as I stay obedient and close to Jesus, I can overcome any circumstance in my life. I see things that I never saw before. God uses me to help others because I am free from being so selfish. The verses memorized during in Teen Challenge are verses that I can recall with the Holy Spirit's help to keep God close during difficult times! They are my hope and promises that I can hold onto daily and provide instructions for right living.

I learned a very important lesson in Teen Challenge; accountability. I have some great people of God who have gone before me in my life. They guide, pray, listen, correct, and most importantly, love me! When I bring things out into the light, God is right there to help. I love the secret things that He shares with me to help others and myself.

Teen Challenge is a true "Jesus boot camp." Trust me, I needed the boot!!! Some called it brainwashing. Well my brain needed washing! After many years of rebelling against my parents and God, I fully surrendered! Teen Challenge helped me to become strong in the battles that I have faced in life since, like a marine in God's Army. It was the most difficult thing that I have ever done in my life, but I knew that if I didn't finish, I was going to die. I truly have the fear of the Lord in my life today. God is not mocked! I knew the truth and He was going to finally set me free indeed, if I just did what was asked of me. I learned to be submissive to authority at Teen Challenge. There were things that I didn't understand, but I knew that the Lord would deliver me from it all; drugs, alcohol, sexual immorality, gambling were all sins that had me in so much bondage.

I am thankful to Jesus for His patience. I knew that for all those years not listening to my parents and their direction, I needed to be re-parented by my Father in heaven! I spent time alone with the Lord so He could heal my wounds, take away all my hurts and replace them with His loving, forgiving, compassionate, and gentle care. It wasn't overnight that I was able to forgive people. It was by working on my sinfulness and wanting forgiveness for myself that I was able to forgive others. But who am I? I am a woman forgiven much who now loves much! I received so much love in my heart that I didn't want others to go to hell. I fell short all my life and if God could still love me and make a way for me to have an eternity with Him, then I can forgive. How? It was a process, a long process! But it was so rewarding that I would do it again! I was able to forgive my abuser! Lord knows what happened to him. I do not want any man to perish and go to hell! I am not the judge. I discovered when I read the scripture that the Lord took the scales off my eyes. They judged Jesus a perfect man and put Him on the cross to die a horrific death! Who are we to judge? I will let the King who loves unconditionally and knows the heart be the judge. I will let Him remove the plank in my eye first!

The first letter I received from my daughter while in Teen Challenge, on the very first line she wrote, "Sometimes, I hate you so much." This was hard to read, but God was right there reminding me that I was forgiven! The devil had no more power over me and I was being protected and shielded under the shadow of His wings!!! I was able to finally stand firm and be there for my daughter. I could read those words and not fall apart. I was strong enough to hear some of the truth in what she was saying and allow her to have her feelings and work through them. As the years went by, she saw that she could finally depend on her mom, that I was truly delivered, and that the Lord had transformed my mind. I was a new creation and the old was really gone, dead and buried! I am no longer a slave to my sins and Jesus is my best friend. I have the Word of God rooted and planted in my life. I have scriptures memorized and I use them to unravel lies and confusion. I know that there is a way out of all my temptations and He who is in me is greater than he who is in the world. Now I am truly able to help others who have had similar experiences as I have had.

Today, my daughter has graduated a two year Christian college and has gone to El Salvador three times to do the Lord's work. She used her own money for another mission's

97

trip as a college student and took a train from Kansas to Los Angles to witness and make meals for the homeless. She is now attending another Christian college and her hope and dreams are to become a counselor for young girls and to teach English as a second language. She is a wonderful daughter and I am so proud of her and thank God for the restoration He has done!

Eleven years have gone by since I first walked into Teen Challenge. For six years now I have owned a CPR and First Aid business that continues to thrive. We keep people alive long enough to get them saved physically and spiritually. I pray for each person that I encounter. I have also been a volunteer EMT for six years now. This position brings me in contact with many addicts. God has placed me there to save lives and encourage others to seek help!

God has restored my life completely. I am so blessed! I frequently read Luke 18: 28-30 where Peter said to Jesus, "We have left all we had to follow you!" Jesus replies, "Truly I tell you, No one who has left home or wife or brothers or sisters or parents or children for the sake of the kingdom of God will fail to receive many times as much in this age, and in the age to come eternal life." Knowing the Lord all of my life, I knew that when I made the decision to surrender all and go to Teen Challenge that the Lord was going to heal and deliver me. I never look back except when I am asked to testify to

others to show His great mercy and restoration power and promises.

As a volunteer with The Red Cross since 2005, God laid it on my heart to help with Hurricane Katrina. I have since deployed to the islands and North Carolina for hurricanes Irma, Maria and Florence. I often pray this prayer, "Lord remove from me any desires in my heart that do not line up with You and please put in my heart Your will." Since praying that, I have moved in the direction I am in and have never been so fulfilled in my life. My family, friends, and life have been restored more than 100% because God protected me from many consequences that could have destroyed me. So many people supported me while I was in Teen Challenge. Remember Carolyn? The disabled woman whom I left stranded many times in my addiction? She would come and visit me at least once a month when I was in Teen Challenge. She is still a part of my life and a very good friend of mine and we attend the same church.

So many people have prayed over my life including my mom, dad, grandma, friends, pastors, and many other people who support Teen Challenge. Thank you everyone! Love is what brought me out of my sin. Grace-filled love from some and love with sternness from others! Love with hard-core truth and reality brought me out of the many lies I believed. God shows me every day and in every situation when I am wrong, need to be more humble, more grateful, and when I need to repent! The Lord is my counselor, The Holy Spirit convicts me when I need it and I need it often! God sent His Son to die for me, and today I thank Him for every single breath I take. I try to be quiet during those times that God is fighting my battles and He is the one who vindicates me. I continue to learn how to trust Him even more!

I now live radically for Jesus, the One who chose to take this hopeless addict and make me whole again when I was once someone thought to be left for dead; never to recover. Thank you, God, for saving me and loving me so much!

Chapter 6
You Must Decide

Ed Boulais

I came into the world on a wintry January 4, 1964. I was born the second of four children to a lower-middle class family in the hills of western Connecticut. As a boy, I remember feeling at times both anger and at other times love from my parents.

While I was young, we lived in a low-income housing neighborhood. Just like neighborhoods today, there were sections of the neighborhood where different ethnic groups would live together. Unfortunately for me, I had to cross a particularly rough section on my way home from my kindergarten class each day. I had been chased and beaten up on more than one occasion leaving me fearful and anxious. Despite the abuse, I never developed the racial prejudice that many of my friends did. My parents taught me that all people are equal and that skin color didn't matter. In fact, my closest neighborhood friends were black and Hispanic.

When I turned six, we moved to a different town in western Connecticut and my parents enrolled me in a Catholic school. The schoolwork was difficult and the priests and the nuns were quite strict. Most transgressions were met with tough discipline, which was a new experience for me. Meanwhile, they taught the Catholic Catechism and lots of facts about God and Jesus Christ.

When I entered second grade, I made my First Communion and then became an altar boy at church. While an altar boy, I experienced things that began to challenge my faith in the Catholic Church. One day, after the priest finished celebrating Mass, another altar boy and I watched as he took the bottle or wine and chugged the whole thing down. This was very disturbing to me. We were only seven years old, but we knew that he wasn't supposed to do that.

By the time I entered sixth grade, I received my Holy Confirmation from a Catholic Bishop. I remember the ornate robe he wore and the special mitre with gold and jewels on his head. He tapped me on the cheek and said, "Receive the Holy Spirit." But afterwards, I didn't feel any different and I continued to question the things I was being taught. On many occasions, I was disciplined and given detention after school. During these detentions, I was made to hold the Bible with outstretched arms for painfully long periods of time. Looking back, I wish they had made me read it instead of simply hold it.

At home, my parents weren't very religious though they said they believed in the Bible and Jesus Christ. They made sure that they took us to church and that my two brothers, my sister, and I had to attend Catholic Catechism classes.

Once I became a teenager, I questioned my faith and the idea of God even more. When I would experience many of the overwhelming feelings and issues that young people face, I wished that God could somehow be a real part of my life and help me deal with my problems. The God I knew about was aloof. I felt like He really didn't care about me because I was rebellious and didn't follow His commandments.

Just before I was to begin high school, my father moved our family to South Florida to start his own business. My parents wanted my older brother and me, to go to a good college and so they sent us to a Catholic prep school that had a strong reputation for both academics and football. I thought that maybe my dream of playing football would come true, but when I tried out freshman year, I quickly found out that even though I was a good player, being 5' 9" and 125lbs was too small to play high school football. I decided to run cross-country and join the wrestling team but I was just an average runner and only participated for two years. Like many teenagers do, I began to experiment, drinking alcohol and smoking weed. I was rather shy and introverted and liked the fact that getting high freed me from my inhibitions and my boring life.

Some would probably have considered me a nerd; I loved learning and did very well in school. Though not the smartest, I worked very hard at my studies and during senior year, I was inducted into the National Honor Society. I received multiple engineering scholarships. I could have chosen Penn State like a couple of my friends, but instead chose the University of Bridgeport, Connecticut not far from where I grew up. Regrettably, I joined the engineering fraternity and spent the first year drinking and partying. As a result, my GPA was too low and so my scholarship was revoked. I tried transferring to a state school but because of my drinking and drug use, I was too high or hung-over to go to class and I ended up flunking out.

After college did not work out, I bounced from job-to-job. I lacked direction in my life and my partying and drug use increased. About this time, the God that I had been taught about in my younger years began to intervene in my life. He worked slowly, over the course of a year and a half, by sending three different people to share the gospel of Jesus Christ with me. This was the first time in my life that I heard the truth about Jesus. All three people said the same thing; Jesus loved me, Jesus had a plan for my life, and I needed to give my life to Him. I still remember the chills I felt as the third person shared with me the exact same words that had been spoken by the first person. I knew that these three people did not know each other and I clearly understood that God was trying to speak to me and rescue me from the path of destruction I was on. Sadly, I didn't respond to God tugging on my heart.

My drinking escalated even more and I began to experience blackouts, I experimented with different kinds of drugs and my life continued to unravel. I became increasingly depressed and anxious and felt an emptiness as my addiction took over. I got arrested a couple of times for driving while intoxicated and ended up getting into a few car accidents. In one of the accidents, I blacked out, my car crossed the yellow line and nearly missed a head-on collision with the car in the other lane. I was travelling at a high rate of speed, my car jumped the curb, snapped a 15 foot tree like a twig, and careened into a brick wall. I smashed my head on the steering wheel and passed out slumped over with the car stuck in drive when I awoke to someone shaking my left arm. I heard a voice that said, "You must decide. You can't keep running from Me. Give me your life and I will set you free." I turned and no one was there. A police officer arrived on scene and I was taken by ambulance to the hospital because of my head injury. Once discharged from the hospital, I was again very depressed. I had no job, no money and my car was totaled. In addition to driving while intoxicated, I also faced other charges from the accident. I felt like there was no way out.

God would not abandon me. Years before my addiction took over, God reached down from heaven and drew my mother into a personal faith in Jesus. And God had used someone I thought very unlikely, a Catholic priest who became born-again. This priest was holding a Bible study and prayer meeting and was proclaiming the gospel of Jesus Christ. He said that he believed Jesus was alive and would work miracles of healing and set people free if they simply prayed and believed God. My mother had heard the message and became the first one in our entire family to embrace personal faith in Jesus.

After my crash and burn, my mother was not harsh or judgmental. She patiently waited for just the right time and after a few days, when she could see I was really low, she told me gently that Jesus loved me and that He could change my life by helping me break free from drinking and drugs. The accident really scared me and I realized that my drinking and drug use were completely out of control and I could end up dead if I didn't stop.

On one particular Friday afternoon, not long after my accident, my mother invited me to attend one of the special services at her church. She said they were broadcasting the service live by satellite. Although I didn't really want to go to church, I decided maybe I should take her up on her offer and investigate what she had told me about. As I got to the church, I realized that I was late and had already missed the 7pm start time. I began to think that maybe I shouldn't go in and that I could give it a try some other time. It was Friday night and I thought that maybe I should see what my friends were doing. I knew I would probably end up drinking and drugging again and just the idea of that happening again scared me. Looking back, I realize that it was the enemy of my soul trying to keep me from turning to the Lord for help. I decided that I couldn't risk it. I told myself that I needed to go and see what this Jesus thing was all about. As I got closer and closer to the church, I began to feel more and more compelled to go in. It was as if something or someone was prompting me and I walked right into the sanctuary.

The place was packed with over a thousand people. I had never seen a church like this and was a bit shocked. I don't remember the message but at the end of the service I was crying like a baby. The pastor asked anyone who wanted to invite Jesus into their heart to stand up to indicate their willingness. I stood to my feet and I asked Jesus to forgive me, come into my heart and change my life. Instantly, I felt as if a million pounds of guilt and shame were lifted. I was free. Jesus had come into my heart and set me free! What an amazing spiritual experience! No drink or drug, no woman or relationship or anything that I ever experienced in my life compared to how I felt when I invited Jesus into my life. I knew that I was forgiven and I had hope in my life again.

I was surprised that I didn't even think about drinking or using drugs. Instead, I just wanted to know the Truth. I began to read the New Testament. I brought my pocket New Testament to work each day and would read it at lunch time. I began to attend a Bible study to learn more about Jesus and God's word. I wondered what God wanted me to do with my life and felt like He had a special plan He wanted me to follow.

After some time, I talked to my pastor about all I had gone through and he said I should pray about going to Bible school. He suggested one in Maine and one in Rhode Island. I decided to visit the one in Rhode Island called Zion Bible College. While there, God made it clear to me that He wanted me to attend. I enrolled and was pleased that they gave me credit for the previous college classes I had completed while pursuing engineering. The academic workload was time consuming but I enjoyed learning about the Bible.

During the spring semester of my junior year, I met a girl from Rhode Island and we began dating. God had also brought her to attend Zion. I finished my degree in the fall. It would be another year before she would graduate and during that time, I returned to western Connecticut to work and seek God's further direction for my life. I decided I would like to marry this girl once she graduated and so I asked her father who was a pastor. He gave us his blessing and I asked her to marry me. She said yes and he agreed to perform the ceremony.

After we were married, we settled in Western Connecticut and began to build our life together. My wife pursued her nursing degree and I worked two jobs. The long hours were very tiring and I was exhausted. Tragically, instead of seeking help and strength from God, I made the horrible decision to start using drugs to "help me" endure the long hours. She had no idea about my struggle and it wasn't long before I was once again falling into the grips of addiction. My life slowly began to spiral out of control.

During this time, we also had decided to start a family. One night, she came home from work and smiled at me as she excitedly declared, "I'm pregnant." I was both overjoyed and scared at the same time. I was happy we were going to have a baby, but scared she would find out about my addiction. I just couldn't stop using drugs. I had every reason to stop, but couldn't; I was not strong enough.

After the birth of our son, we moved to eastern Tennessee where my parents were now living after their retirement. My mother had agreed to help watch our son while my wife completed her nursing degree. During this time I continued to hide my addiction and struggled to hold our marriage together. The downhill slide continued for about four

111

years until one tragic night; I overdosed and ended up in the hospital. Drugs had stopped my heart. Later, when I awoke, the doctor informed me what had happened. Twice my heart had stopped and the doctor and nurses tried different drugs to get it to beat again without success. Running out of time, the doctor used the electric paddles two times to shock my heart. Nothing. As the doctor was about to give up, the nurse asked to shock me one last time. Reluctantly, the doctor shocked my heart again and it re-started.

When I awoke, I realized I would have to face my wife with the truth about my addiction. Just as I suspected, she was crushed. After a short time, she said she was taking our son and returning to Massachusetts to live with her father. I thought perhaps moving away and returning to New England would give me a fresh start and help me to shake my addiction. I was wrong. We returned to Massachusetts, but I still couldn't stop using drugs.

Finally, she'd had enough and she told me that she was divorcing me. I found myself homeless, living out of my car. These were the darkest, most miserable days of my life. Depressed doesn't even come close to describing how I felt. Alone. I was alone. I was afraid of overdosing and also afraid of being sick from not using drugs. Something had to give or it was going to be over for me for good.

The assistant pastor at the church I was attending

suggested I try Teen Challenge to help me get free from my addiction. I thought about it and decided to pray about going there. I called Teen Challenge and left a message that I needed to talk to someone about entering the program. A thousand thoughts were flowing through my mind. What if they won't accept me? What if the program is too difficult? What if I can't see my son? Later that day, a guy from Teen Challenge admissions returned my call and informed me what I needed to do to be able to come into the program. I was really uneasy about the whole idea, but decided to give it a try. I asked the assistant pastor if he could drop me off at the program in Brockton, Massachusetts. He agreed to bring me the following week.

I arrived at Teen Challenge Massachusetts (Brockton) full of both anxiety and fear; anxiety about the difficulties I would face and fear of the unknown. I was also very depressed about being separated from my wife and son. My whole life had disintegrated into brokenness and pain. I remember feeling like the rug had been pulled right out from under my feet. After a few days had passed, during prayer time after dinner, I went into the chapel to pray. I walked over to the wall, closed my eyes, and just started talking to God. I was feeling overwhelmed. I cried out and told Him I was dying from addiction and my life was in pieces. I had lost my wife, my son, my job, my car, and even my health. The only thing left was that I had going for me is that I was still breathing. I had squandered all the blessings He had given me. I had not listened to Him. I asked Him to forgive me. I pleaded with Him to break the chains of addiction. I asked Him to love me. I wanted to live! I broke down and began to weep and sob. It felt as if Jesus had wrapped His arms around me. When I opened my eyes, I knew I couldn't play games with God anymore. I also knew I was forgiven. I knew that God had heard me and that He had set me free. I knew that I could no longer trust myself and that I had to trust God if I wanted to live. I knew that He really did love me and would help me.

The name Teen Challenge really is fitting because I wrestled through many "challenges" as I began to progress through the program. I realized God was there and He had my attention. In my brokenness, I was able to begin healing—from the inside out. God used the leaders and pastors almost daily to speak life and healing into me. For the first time in my life, I learned the real value and reason for humility and serving others. Perhaps most important of all, I was finally free from addiction and free from my past. It was such a new beginning to finally be free to follow God's plans for my life. A few months into the program, I was assigned to work in the Academic Center to monitor and assist the men as they worked through their lessons and issue-specific books. A short time later the Lord spoke to my heart during one of the chapel services while I was praying. He said that one day I would be the head of the Academic Center. I was both greatly humbled that God could use me despite the scars and brokenness in my life and at the same time I was honored. One day, while reviewing a resident's work in the classroom, it hit me that the reason God led me to attend and complete Bible school was that He wanted me to do ministry at Teen Challenge. I had finally come full circle to the place where God wanted me. Finally, I was actually "doing" God's plan, instead of mine.

Today, it has been over seven years since I came to Teen Challenge. The day before I graduated, a supervisor came to me saying they wanted me to serve as the leader of the Academic Center. It has been a great honor and privilege to serve the Lord while serving the men and ministry of Teen Challenge Massachusetts (Brockton) where I have had the great privilege to sit and share the gospel of Jesus with over a thousand men and watch their lives change. God truly is faithful and I look forward to seeing Jesus continue to work His miracles setting men free from the chains of addiction. He who the Son sets free shall be free indeed!

Chapter 7
Expect a Miracle

Dave Webb

It was a rainy day in Memphis, Tennessee cloudy and gloomy. My girlfriend was a fulltime student at a college in the downtown area and I was a senior in high school. I picked her up this particular afternoon, yet it wasn't a usual rendezvous. We would normally be joyous to see each other, smiles, kisses, full of news of our day; but not on this day. We rode on in silence, and in no rush to get to where we were going. The drive to our destination, only a few miles from where I picked her up, seemed like a lifetime, and as we got nearer, we were both sinking with every passing moment of the drive.

We passed the old Memphis Greyhound bus station, and there it was: an old building seeming sterile and lifeless. The Memphis Center for Reproductive Health, the first Planned Parenthood in Memphis, opened a few months before we walked through the doors. Roe vs. Wade the historic landmark decision legalizing abortion had just passed. It was 1974 I had just turned 17 and my girlfriend just turned 18, and we were going to do the unthinkable. Walking through those doors that day would haunt me for the next 32 years and give Satan a foothold in my life!

Even though our relationship went on for another year, it was never the same and we drifted painfully apart. We could barely talk about it with each other and were too ashamed to share it with family and friends. I had experimented with drugs for years in my early teens and I had sold a pound of weed to have the abortion, but from that day on the goal was to do as much drugs as I could so I could bury the pain. Within weeks, I was drinking every day and within a couple of months I turned to barbiturates, then Dilaudid, and then morphine. By the fall of 1975, I was a full-blown "drug abuser" doing anything and everything to bury my self-inflicted pain. Soon acid and cocaine were also a normal regiment in my life. My behavior changed as I went from a happy drinker to being a mean drunk. Blackouts became common with my typical "day after calls" apologizing to everyone even though not knowing what transpired the night before. Many of my friends grew sick of it and did everything to stay away.

With this came trouble with the law. A DWI arrest and drug arrests put me in front of the same judge several times until the winter of 1976. My downward trajectory was rapid and took no prisoners other than me! By Christmas 1976 I knew I was in trouble and in February 1977 I dropped out of college for the second time. I had no semblance of joy or happiness, and was facing the same judge now for the fourth time! This was going to land me some time and really bury my future, so my father spoke to the judge with whom he went to high school and a "deal" was struck in the form of mercy. The judge recommended I leave Memphis by way of the military immediately! So from the courtroom my father drove me to the nearest recruiting station, and a month later I was in the Army headed to Fort Dix, New Jersey, bound for more trouble!

Before I get into that, I need to share my family history. My father, William Morton Webb was a big man, but gentle. He was from Memphis, Tennessee and when he was 18 years old joined the Air Force with his nephew Eddie. He served in the Korean War in 1950-1951 and in the Vietnam War in 1969-1970. I am proud of my father's service and how he loved and took care of us. We never lacked and when he was around he had time for us. He was a pillar of all the communities we lived in as an Air Force family, a deacon in the Southern Baptist Church, a president of the PTA, and coached both my brother Richard and me in baseball, football, and basketball. At an early age he taught us the Word of God and led by example. Though he never saw me living life as a Christian, I see his footsteps along my life's path right behind my Lord's

119

footprints, I hear his voice singing the old hymns; these have been guiding examples to lead me to Christ. He died of a massive heart attack at the age of 52, ten years after he retired from the Air Force and three weeks after shooting one of his best rounds of golf! There has been a hole our family nothing has been able to fill for the past 35 years. A major regret I have is from the time I was 17, he rarely saw me sober!

My dad met my mother in Japan in 1955. Yuko Takeda was a five-foot tall Japanese woman with an immediate and empowering presence that made it sometimes seem as though she was seven feet tall! In my dad's absence while he was in the service, she did her best taking care of us. She never drove, that was tough at times. We did a lot of walking. I never knew it until I was into my teens, but my mother was eight years older than my father. She had seen the devastation of WW2 on her hometown of Sendai and lost three brothers to the war. She also lost relatives in Sendai and Tokyo to massive bombing raids, and at Hiroshima when the atomic bomb was dropped. She carried some deep scars and wounds that would become evident at times within the family. She showed little love and at times was very verbally abusive toward my brother, my sister, and me; and at times the abuse became physical. Yet this was the person with whom I spent most of my formative years. So while I felt little love growing up, I sensed that I had to earn her approval. Although she had "received Christ" into her life when I was five, I saw little fruit of it. I was sure that the enemy still had a firm grip on my mom!

I went to Fort Dix for my basic training in the US Army and became a motivated soldier earning the rank of private E-2 in eight weeks of basic training. I then went to my advanced training at the Engineering Corp Brigade at Fort Belvoir, Virginia and met my soon-to-be wife. Upon completing our training we learned that she was going to Hawaii and I was going to Ft. Hood Texas. I filed joint domicile to be able to serve in Hawaii with her. December of 1977 we married in the newlywed capital of the world, and quickly found out it how expensive it was to live there. Hawaii got even tougher when she got pregnant. The honeymoon was over!

Once pregnant, she opted out of the service and got out of her obligation, with an Honorable Discharge. We were both doing drugs and drinking too much and it wasn't long before I got busted. I lost my rank and was thrown in Pearl Harbor Confinement center, found guilty by a military for failure to report, striking a superior officer, and conspiring to sell a class one drug. Within six months of landing in Hawaii I was married, had a pregnant wife, was busted from an E-3 to an E-1, and found guilty of three charges by a military court, facing three to five years in Leavenworth, Kansas.

It seemed hopeless so I told my wife to leave me, forget about me, I had no means to provide for her and no way out of this hopeless situation. What I didn't know was the Lord had a plan for our lives, a plan that I couldn't even explain! I asked to speak to the prison chaplain because I was told he could show me how to get help for my pregnant wife, since I wasn't getting paid at the time. After ministering to me and sharing he would do all he could to help my wife, he read a verse from the Bible in Isaiah 58:11, "And the Lord will guide you continually and satisfy your desire in scorched places and make your bones strong; and you shall be like a watered garden, like a spring of water, whose waters do not fail." He then read out of Jeremiah 1:5, "Before I formed you in the womb I knew you, and before you were born I consecrated you; I appointed you a prophet to the nations." That scripture took me back to the abortion I had and I told the chaplain to get out of my face and I didn't want to hear anymore. The guilt and shame that came over me was like a flood trying to drown me out and choke me. As the chaplain walked away he turned and said, "Jesus is calling you and has plans for your life. Set your eyes on Him and He will help you break the chains and freely soar!" I sank in my guilt and despair hoping I would die right there in that tiny cell. I felt so alone.

At the same time Christ was revealing Himself in my life and to my wife. She had gone to see the chaplain and he shared with her all we had talked about. He connected her with resources for military families to help with travel expenses, food, clothing, etc., yet the best resource he gave her was the church. He told her to come to a prayer meeting and meet the people there. Well, what happened next was a miracle as the Holy Spirit moved on her life as she repented and received Christ right there and then, was baptized, and received the baptism of the Holy Spirit! She found family away from her hometown of Philadelphia and the people loved her, accepted her, and began to pray for me. They were praying a prayer of miraculous freedom and release and that God would show His favor on me.

Several weeks after my initial visit with the chaplain, he came back and told me to expect a miracle. What did that mean? Why would he say that to a wretched individual like me? Why me? Who am I? Questions came pouring in. The thought, that a murderer like me, after killing my innocent baby could have favor with the Almighty!

The next day Marine guards came for me and said to gather my belongings; I was leaving. I thought I was flying to Kansas to spend the next few years of my life in a prison, but then an Army sergeant came in to get me and said, "Are you rcady for your next assignment?" I asked him what he meant. He introduced himself and said I would be attached to his unit in the 25th Division Artillery. I would work in the motor pool doing a totally different job. In the vehicle, I met another sergeant. Little did I know how much of an impact he would

123

have in my life!

I had been fully released! God moved abundantly in our lives. My record was expunged the next year, Nick was born on October 31, 1978, and eleven months later my son David was born on October 6, 1979. I was restored my rank and made E-4 and was on the E-5 list. We saw God move again when He healed my wife of cancer during her second pregnancy with David. I was reassigned to a Military Intelligence unit on Schofield Barracks and went to some extraordinary places such as New Zealand and attached to an MP unit in Thailand at the Red Cross camp on the Cambodian border. I separated with an Honorable Discharge, received an ARCOM (Army Commendation Medal) and a MSM (Meritorious Service Medal). While I owed it all to my Lord and Savior Jesus Christ, something was still plaguing me, following me. Like the color of my hair or the scar on my back, the abortion would follow me the next 26 years of my life!

Once out of the Army, we decided to try making a life in Philadelphia. After being laid off several times and finding myself in trouble with methamphetamines, we decided to move to New Hampshire. Things seemed good, but three years later my father grew ill and my mother asked if we could move down to Memphis to help her out. After my father passed I began drinking heavily. I couldn't deal with his loss and the pain of the abortion. Seeing once again my mother's inability to love brought back the pain of my childhood and I battled God with so many unanswered questions about her abuse. All the while battling that, it seemed every place we went, even every church we went to, talked about abortion and they were calling it murder! They were asking people to protest in front of the Planned Parenthood offices and I just could not be a part. They were opening counter clinics offering ultrasounds and I was asked to help fundraise, but I just couldn't get involved. I felt frozen, like I couldn't move my feet. Nobody around me, friends or family knew the pain I was going through. I felt alone, as I had no real relationship with Jesus Christ. The sin of abortion continued to haunt me, and little did I know all I needed to do was bring it to Christ. I felt as though He died on the cross for everyone's sins, but mine!

Once my mother was settled after my father's passing, we moved back to New Hampshire. By this time I had my electrical license, so getting work anywhere was easy I played the "Hokey Pokey" in my relationship with Jesus. You know, "I put my left foot in, I put my left foot out, I put my left foot in, and shake it all about." I took more out than I put in! You get the picture. My Christian walk was not a walk it was a show. I was showing some change on the outside, but God requires change on the inside. I was good at hiding my outside behaviors, but in Matthew 15:8 Jesus quotes Isaiah, "These people draw near to Me with their mouth, And honor

125

Me with their lips, But their heart is far from Me. And in vain they worship Me, Teaching as doctrines the commandments of men." Proverbs 23:26 says, "My son, give Me your heart, and let your eyes observe My ways." Romans 12:2, "And do not be conformed to this world, but be transformed by the renewing of your mind, that you may prove what is that good and acceptable and perfect will of God." There are many more scriptures that reveal God commands an inside out change.

Between my wife's struggle with mental illness for many years and a job slump in New England in the early 90's, we had more than we could cope with in our marriage. We would let God in and then push Him out. Let Him in, then push Him out. We went to counseling, but I was in no way able or equipped to deal with my wife's illness. We sought counseling from several pastors, but my wife's secular counselor suggested she leave me, so she did. I was angry with God for this and rebelled.

The only good things in my life were my children: Nick, David Jr., Michelle, and Melissa. I was what the judge called, "the lesser of two evils" between my wife and I, so I got custody of all four teenagers. Sixteen, 15, 14, and 13, full of life and all that teenagers do! I also had another child in 1996. What a wonderful little girl Breanna was and a great addition to our lives, but her mother and my relationship ended as my addiction went to another level. My two sons soon followed in my path and were beginning to experiment with drugs. Nick was playing a more dangerous game doing opiates. I confronted him about his drug use and he told me I should "look in the mirror." He was right and that was a punch in the gut. I felt like such a hypocrite. I was once again doing cocaine and prescription opiates on top of drinking. I realized my addiction was getting out of control, so I locked myself in a hotel room for five days and detoxed myself. It was a battle, but the addiction wasn't the core issue; sin, selfishness, lack of love, and guilt and shame were. Those were the heart issues I could not face!

After my children graduated and moved out of the house, I took a once in a lifetime engineering job in New Hampshire and moved shortly after my youngest left the house. I got married again, but my past was close behind. Before I knew it I was in a rehab in New Hampshire and then several months later I wound up in a rehab in Connecticut. Within one year I was in four rehabs! This was too much on my marriage and we separated, yet all that time God was still right there looking over me, in my selfishness, my sin, and my squander, He never left mc alone.

Now once again in legal trouble, I lost my driver's license, which is an important tool starting a new business for yourself. Breaking probation often I found myself in jail. Facing the judge at the age of 46, he told me that I should max out my time so that when I got out I would have no probation. So I did just that and during that whole time I sensed God calling me back to Him.

Once out of jail I saw my path would lead me either back to prison or death! I was using more than ever and my addiction took a turn for the worse, as if that were possible. In October 2005 I was renting an RV in the back of my dealer's house! How convenient was that! If I worked, I would give my money to the man and get what I needed. I tried to stay off the booze, but it didn't work. March 2006 I was right back in court looking at doing time, needing real change in my life, because I was out of control with no direction. I went to Maine to see an old college buddy, and he set me up with a job interview and pushed to get me into a nice manufacturing facility. I was hired on the spot for a sweet job and excellent pay as a heat-treat engineer. I asked for a couple of weeks to settle my business in Vermont, pack my stuff and move up.

All ready to move up to Waldoboro, Maine after selling my stuff, I decided to stop one last time at a favorite bar in town on a Friday evening about 6:30pm. The next thing I knew it is 7:00am Monday, and I was in a hotel in Brattleboro, Vermont with less than two dollars on me of the forty two hundred I had started with Friday night! I was so down and felt so ashamed. What a loser I am, so I pulled my shotgun out of the back of my SUV and decided to do it, to end my life, but I had no shells. I went to a New Hampshire store that sold guns and ammo.

I was such a mess I went in and asked the clerk to sell me one shell. He didn't sell them that way and he could tell I was in trouble. I was desperate and told him I needed it to kill a woodchuck in my backyard and only had a couple of dollars, but he could tell I was not in my right mind. I then began to argue with him and even started crying. He asked me to leave or he would call the police! Walking out I was at a place lower than I had ever been. I felt shackled and all alone. My family, my children, and my friends had left me and wanted no more to do with me.

I went out to my car feeling so ashamed. I couldn't even find a way to end my life! I couldn't even do that right! When I got to my vehicle and turned it on, a Christian radio program came on. A well-known Christian music artist shared his testimony and it spoke so clearly to me. It was as if Christ was speaking directly to me, three simple words, "I love you!" Leaving the parking lot I took a left instead of a right. God directed me to some longtime friends I had not seen for 10 years. When I got to their home in Winchester, New Hampshire, Carol and her family welcomed me with open arms and loved on me and prayed over me. They called their pastor, an old friend of mine and he came over to pray for me. As they were praying they both said, "Teen Challenge!" Much to my surprise because I was no teen, I was 48 years old!

April of 2006 I went into the beautiful Teen Challenge Johnson, Vermont center. God knew exactly what I needed to begin to deal with my addiction and the very reasons I continued to make the decisions I had made for so many years. The leaders there began to pour into me and I sensed that God was going to reveal to me His plan for my life. Pastor Rick Welch was so instrumental in his servant leadership model. He showed me what grace was and we hit it off immediately. He, like myself, came into the program at an older age, and his example of what God can do in transforming individuals stood out. There were many others there that prayed for me. Mike Duarte and Lloyd Alcon were very instrumental in my discipleship process. They helped me grow and made me accountable.

After being there a few weeks we went to Camp Champion in New York and what an experience that was! All the people there; residents, leaders, pastors and their families, overwhelmed me. And I began to see that these leaders had been once in the very spot I was in. It gave me so much hope and endurance, which I am sure helped me to finish. Pastor Jimmy Jack took the podium and began to preach and share his life and testimony. As he talked, I don't even know what he said, but he gave an invitation. Just before that, it was as if he pointed at me, as if Christ was speaking through him to say, "David, it's time to let it go. It's time to fully give your life to me in surrender. It's time to make me Lord of your life!" At that moment the weight of 32 years of guilt and shame, 32 years of walking alone in pain, 32 years of selfishness and pride began to shed off! The lifetime of not knowing a mother's love and her abuse started peeling off of me! The guilt of that abortion on that rainy, cloudy, and gloomy day in Memphis was being lifted! Leaders around me began to pray for me as guilt after guilt, shame after shame, sin after sin was nailed to the cross! For the first time I felt the darkness fall off of me. I praise God for His love and healing that He poured out on me that day and every day since! I began to realize that God's faithfulness is great, even when mine is in doubt! When I am not faithful He is! From then on I began to sit in God's love every day, to walk in the victory, and in the assurance that Christ goes before me.

I was blessed to go on a Teen Challenge mission trip with 15 other residents and leaders. We went to Nuevo Laredo, Mexico, one of the worst cities in Mexico on the Interstate 35 corridor with many murders, drug gangs, and turf wars. The local government was very corrupt and broken! This was the experience God used to compel upon me to share my life and testimony with others and to bring the Gospel of Jesus Christ to a sick, dying, and addicted world. I learned that it isn't up to what I feel about myself, but to be willing to do and to go wherever He wishes. God can and will use me in any venture He chooses. Some of the poorest of the poor showered love on us and gave us their best. Church after church came to hear us speak and many gave their lives to Christ. I witnessed that joy and riches do not come in the things we possess, but in Christ! I learned that my life was not my own, but if I lose my life for Christ I will gain it! It was the trip of a lifetime where many friendships developed along with a sense of commitment first to Christ, then to one another.

My experiences in the Massachusetts center, for the leadership phase were extraordinary! I was on a maintenance team that helped me grow in faith. I trusted God to meet all of my all needs. We didn't always have the funds to do what we needed to do, but somehow God always made a way! I learned to trust God by faith rather than sight and that God moves in the supernatural and we often can't see Him moving, but He always comes through. I took these wonderful tools with me when I commenced in July 2007 and graduated in January of 2008. However, of all the things I got out during my time there was to daily pray and grow in my relationship with Christ, to read the Word of God daily and journal my way through, and to get up when I fall. "For though a righteous man fall seven times, they rise again, but the wicked stumble in times of calamity." Proverbs 24:16

Today my life is transformed through the life-saving

blood of Jesus Christ! I have had to forgive myself and repent for the abortion of years ago. I am now an advocate for life and for the child in the womb. I have also become a part of a post abortion trauma-healing group. Forgiving my mother has brought such healing and freedom for me. As I share some of the things I went through as a child with those that have gone through similar circumstances, I think about my mother and realize she loved with the only ability she knew how.

I am married to a godly and faithful woman of God, Maria, a "Proverbs 31" woman who shares with me a passion for the lost and hurting. God has blended us, Maria is more contemplative and thorough, and I am a "let's jump in and see where we land" kind of approach! It seems to work! God has also blessed me with another child, Cayli, now seven. She has made me young again, at least in my heart! Through Christ alone I have gained the trust of my children, my grandchildren, my brother and sister, and many friends I have made around the world. Life in Christ is more adventurous than anything I did without Him. I can walk in the power of the Holy Spirit and the fullness of the spiritual gifts. I now teach and preach in prisons, churches, the streets, and anywhere God will lead. So many things I learned in Teen Challenge; God's forgiveness, grace and mercy, His healing and delivering power, and that Christ will use the foolish things of this world to confound the wise! All the places I went and journeys He has blessed

133

me with while I was there; Camp Champion, missions trip to Mexico, working the Nascar races at Loudon, Brockton, New Jersey, Fitchburg, and of course my Teen Challenge home in Vermont, I attribute it all to the power of the cross and Jesus Christ who has saved me and delivered me from Satan's grip. He has pulled me out of the muck and miry clay, cleaned me off, and said, "I go before you, follow My lead." Just like Job, "My former state was ordinary, but my future will be extraordinary!" Teen Challenge is a gift to me. It's Christ who saved me and He used the conduit of Teen Challenge to introduce the very things I needed to make Him Lord of my life, and I will forever be grateful! But most of all, Teen Challenge showed me love, the love of Christ that can't be measured, a love that can't be stopped! God's love drives out fear and has taught me to love others better!

I stood on this scripture in Teen Challenge and I still stand on it today:

"For I am convinced, that neither death nor life, neither angels nor demons, neither things present nor in the future, nor any power; nor height nor depth, nor anything in creation, can separate us from the love of God which is in Christ Jesus our Lord." Romans 8:38-39

I can't boast about my love for God because I fail Him daily, but I can boast about His love for me because He is faithful and never fails me!

134

Chapter 8
"I'm Gonna Pray for Your Restoration"

Steve Hager

I have experienced God. I have seen Him supernaturally deliver me from countless addictions in an instant. I watched Him restore my sanity, wholeness and clarity, and He has changed my mind about who I am and what I thought was possible for my life. Much of this transformation took place on Stanton Mountain Road in Lebanon, New Jersey; one of my favorite places on earth. That is where I finally met Jesus. In case you're wondering what is on Stanton Mountain Road, it is the 88-acre campus of Teen Challenge New Jersey, where I spent my second round of drug rehabilitation.

Here is the story as I remember it leading me to drug rehabilitation.

I was born in 1981, raised by loving parents in a small town called Bayville in New Jersey. In the early years growing up, I always felt safe, secure, and loved. I was a good kid with straight "A"'s on my report cards. We didn't go to church, but I believed in God. I loved my grandparents, my sister, my pets, sports, and collected baseball cards. One night when I was 13, I woke up to my mom and grandmother talking. I eavesdropped on their conversation and I found out that my hero, my dad, had taken off to go live with another woman, a very young woman at that. She was 17 years old.

The days after finding this out are a blur, but two things that I remember took place: a conversation with my dad where I didn't have the guts to tell him how I felt and I started smoking cigarettes.

I soon discovered the electric guitar and alternative rock music. I was hooked. I played guitar all the time My friends were all the freaks, skaters, and metal heads, and they all liked me because I was actually pretty good at guitar. I started a band. I remember going to what my parents called "a born-again" church with my drummer's family. I got into it when I was there and even considered going up to the altar to get saved, but was too shy. I thought at the time I wasn't good enough for God to love me. My drummer friend also helped me discover marijuana. I totally hated the feeling of being high. I felt like I committed an unpardonable sin and everybody knew it. I was totally paranoid and filled with fear and guilt. Yet, I still decided to smoke weed daily until I could deal with it. Finally, I felt that I fit in and weed enabled me to feel like I had gained the acceptance I needed at the time.

I also didn't like alcohol at first, but I continued to drink until eventually it became fun. The bass player in my first band I met in high school. Surprisingly, his parents were "born-again" missionaries, and they took me to church once as well. Again, it sounded good, but I still wasn't saved. So I got him started smoking weed. I remember meeting one of his parents' friends who told me, "You are very talented. One day you will be making music for the kingdom of God." I didn't realize at the time that this was prophetic. I thought the guy was a first class lunatic.

Weed, music, and alcohol got me through high school. I did say my first sinner's prayer in a grocery store parking lot at age 16 while I was high on weed. Two evangelists shared the gospel with me and sold me on it, but my heart was still hurt and wickedness was more appealing.

I made it into college on a music scholarship and started getting serious about a career in music. I practiced a lot learning both classical and jazz guitar. I got a job as a guitar teacher making great money. During this time, I was a "hippie" and would go to jam band festivals and take a lot of different drugs (ecstasy, molly, acid, mushrooms, DMT, etc.). I enjoyed altering my consciousness while listening to music. I also was into Eastern religion and philosophy (Taoism, Buddhism, Hinduism, etc.), it all seemed cool to me at the time.

Yet, it brought me a lot of spiritual confusion and unanswered questions, which led me to church again. I got "re-saved" and went four weeks in a row. I even brought two friends who also got saved. Yet, not one of us kept going.

Around this time I was making a name for myself in the local music scene and had some small music success. Everybody thought I'd be famous; at least that was my perception. I started doing cocaine because it made me more rock and roll. For a year, all I cared about was cocaine. I realized it was ruining my life so I quit. Two weeks after that, I met a girl. The night we met we were high on ecstasy, but we fell in love, moved in together, and had a baby. Up until the pregnancy, we would take Percocet pills (an opiate) to relax and have fun. Not all the time, just recreationally. I felt like a responsible adult, no more cocaine, just an occasional pill. When she got pregnant, that stopped, except twice, and both times I passed out, which never happened before. Once, I smashed my face on the ground.

My daughter Elliot was born on February 19, 2007. She was amazing. She was beautiful. She was a gift from the Lord and I knew it. They prescribed her mother Percocet pills for her pain. She took them all, got a refill, and took them all. After her refills ran out, she found them from a friend of mine. At this point, I decided I couldn't stop her so I would join her. This led us into a pill addiction. We stole a prescription pad from her job as a dental assistant. We wrote and filled two fraudulent prescriptions a day for months. One for us to take, and one to sell. As drug dealers, we entered the next level. I had so much guilt that my beautiful daughter wasn't enough to make me quit. I was bound to drugs, and I hated myself. Every day I said I would quit and every day I caved in. I was a bad man and a bad father. Eventually we developed a tolerance to the pills and moved to stronger doses. Then I discovered Suboxone. My doctor was not very encouraging. He told me that I would be an addict and may need to be on Suboxone for life. He also prescribed me Klonopin for my anxiety. I was heavily dependent on both for six years. Since Suboxone fell short in getting me high I would mix it with Adderall, and the combo would get me there. I would also drink and smoke weed. My life was out of control. I was now working as a bartender in Asbury Park, New Jersey and I was taking Suboxone, Klonopin, Adderall, whiskey, and weed daily all while trying to provide for and support a family. I was unsure of myself as a man and thought my fiancé was cheating on me. I felt bad for my daughter and my fiancé that they were stuck with me. I thought if I died they would be so much better off.

I got a strange phone call one day from an old friend, the bass player from my band who I mentioned earlier. He said, "The Holy Spirit told me I need to call you and tell you that you need help. I know you're not doing well and I think you should go to Teen Challenge."

This was the craziest thing I ever heard. I immediately lied and told him how great I was doing and that he was wrong.

Three weeks later I entered Teen Challenge.

Suboxone withdrawal was terrible. For 26 nights I barely slept more than an hour or two, but on day 27, I was free. The Holy Spirit began a work in me and the scriptures were coming to life. I was so free. It was heaven on earth. Then my grandma died. I loved her so much and hated that she died knowing I was in rehab. God comforted me, but the doubts started creeping in. Then on my first visit, my fiancé showed me her track marks. She had started shooting heroin after I left.

After seven weeks, I decided that I would leave Teen Challenge and help her get clean. I thought I was strong enough. All my leaders told me I wasn't, making me mad, resentful, and ready to prove them all wrong.

Six months after leaving Teen Challenge, I shot heroin for the first time in my life. They were right. I sold every guitar I owned. I sold other people's guitars that I borrowed, and I used every penny that I made to buy heroin for us. This went on for three months until we moved in with my dad and he helped us find a doctor who put me back on Suboxone. We both went back on Suboxone because she was pregnant again. I got a job selling cars, we got a new apartment, a car, and had the baby, another beautiful girl. One day I ran out of Suboxone. I called my friend and asked if I could borrow one from her. She said yes, but you have to come to church with me. I went and it brought me to tears. I remembered the freedom, the peace, the beautiful seven weeks I had, and I ran to the front for prayer. I asked if they would pray for me to get off of Suboxone.

What happened the next day was completely unbelievable. I relapsed and shot heroin. I also brought some home and gave it to my fiancé. We were back in the game only this time we found new ways to get money. I started selling heroin and my fiancé advertised on craigslist ad that she would do sexual favors for men for money. I knew about it, allowed it, and encouraged it. I lost all respect for myself as a man and really wanted to die. I would shoot double the amount anyone else would and shake my fist at God the next morning that He didn't let me overdose.

The Department of Child Services found out about me and took my kids away. Their mother was able to keep them because she shot her dope in a place that left no track marks and knew how to trick the drug tests using our own daughter's urine. They stayed in a welfare motel in Seaside, New Jersey and I was basically homeless. Though my dad would let me crash at his house, I had to get there after 10 pm and leave before 6 am. I went to a five-day detox to get clean so I could be around my kids, but I shot up one hour after I got home.

My mom was strong and amazing through all of this. It was Christmas 2014 and I asked her to help me with gifts for my daughters. I got them everything on their list and snuck into the motel so we could spend Christmas together. Shortly after I got there, the police showed up. I tried hiding in the shower, but they found me. They offered to let me go and not bring me to jail if I could find a ride out of Seaside. No one would take my calls and I was out of friends, so I offered to walk. It was a seven-mile walk that morning. I was all out of dope, all out of cigarettes, had no battery life on my phone in the cold New Jersey winter.

As I started across the bridge that connects Seaside and Toms River, I was getting pelted with water, sand, and wind. I decided at that moment to start a conversation with God. I poured out my heart to God as I walked across the bridge. I told him how badly I blew it and that I would give Him my life since I wanted to die anyway. I was broken and I knew all along there would only be one way to fix me. I had so much damage on the inside of me that the only One wise enough and qualified enough to repair me had to be the One who created me; Almighty God.

I believe Jesus walked across that bridge with me that Christmas afternoon.

Although I had an encounter, I continued to use the drugs because I just couldn't stop. My dad let me stay with him. One day while at his house, I saw on Facebook that the Teen Challenge choir was a few miles away. I asked if they could pick me up and bring me back with them. That wasn't an option at the time, but they put me in contact with Admissions. After the phone interview, the Admissions Coordinator asked if he could pray for me. When he was praying I felt God's love and I wept. No one had asked to pray for me for anything since my first visit to Teen Challenge.

The program was at capacity, but they made an exception for me and allowed me to stay on an air mattress. Praise God because I would've been dead if it wasn't for that air mattress. My first time in prayer I received my restoration and deliverance. We were praying in groups of three when another resident at the program, a larger African American man put his hand over my heart and asked, "What do you want me to pray for?" I said, "Pray that my kids are safe while I'm here." He said, "No. What do you really want me to pray for?" I asked him to pray that I don't have bad withdrawals. He said, "No. You need restoration. I am going to pray for your restoration." And he started praying like I had never heard before, Holy Spirit praying, quoting scripture, very thorough, and elaborate with emotion and power. Since after that prayer, I have never again struggled with my addiction to substances.

145

Changed Lives

God supernaturally delivered me! Later that night, I laid on my air mattress and made a commitment to God. I'll give you these 15 months to change me, to show me You are real, and to heal me. I decided that no matter what, I would finish. I was determined.

Two weeks into the program, I found out my fiancé tried to hang herself in the hotel room with the kids sleeping in the same room. The kids were moved to foster care, and she was moved to a psychiatric unit. The Teen Challenge leaders said, "I know you're probably thinking of leaving." I cut them short and said, "No. This is where I need to be right now."

As I learned more of God's Word and spent time alone looking into the mountains, God would speak so clearly to me. I learned to hear His voice and gained some amazing wisdom in such a short amount of time. I had realized that the Spirit of God was living inside of me. I was free from fear. I believed that God really loved me and sent His Son to die so that I could know Him. The drama and work of the program and missing the worldly things had no adverse effect on my mind. I was obsessed and in love with Jesus. I knew I would have my kids back. I knew I would be the man I always knew I could be. I learned how I was fearfully and wonderfully made in the image of God. That God had a plan to prosper me and I was able to look at my past through a new filter. I was forgiven. I could see and even expose the strategies of the enemy. My eyes were open. The world was colorful and beautiful again. Every breath felt like my first breath. I had no money, was in some ways what the world would consider a failure, but I was surrounded by God's love. The people around me genuinely cared and were really trying and succeeded at showing love. I was in awe of God. I started worshipping, playing, and singing songs about the Lord. He spoke to me in prayer one morning. He said, "For years you have made music for my enemy. Where has it gotten you?" I looked in the sky and I promised God I would only make music for Him. That crazy prophet knew this when I was a teenager!

Today, I am a worship leader at Redemption Church in Knoxville, Tennessee. Every week we lead people into the presence of God, break chains, break yokes, and offer peace and healing through music.

While at Teen Challenge, I asked the Lord about my relationship with my fiancé. I knew it was co-dependent, and she was my kryptonite. But I knew I could never leave her on my own strength. I had no peace. I prayed that God would give me a sign if I needed to break it off or stay with her. The next day, I called her and out of nowhere she told me that she cheated on me and was living with another man. I thanked her for telling me and hung up the phone. Under any normal circumstances my heart should've been broken. But God gives such peace and comfort. I cried that night, but there

147

was no pain. God was moving mountains for me.

One day at Teen Challenge, I met with the case manager for DCS about the custody of my children. He asked what my plan was. I answered, "I am going to seek God first, and everything else will fall into place." I didn't know when I said it if he were an atheist or a believer. Turns out he was a believer. We talked about the Lord the rest of the interview. I had nothing but favor when it came to getting custody of my kids.

I graduated Teen Challenge in May 2016 and I moved to Knoxville, Tennessee. In June 2016, I was awarded full custody of my children and the DCS case was dropped. I landed an amazing job working at a car dealership where we have regular prayer meetings and Bible study. I am making twice as much money as I ever have in my life and now have good credit. Many months I am the top salesman, and I have met and witnessed to many people while on the job.

My first Wednesday night in Knoxville, I went to church. I had plans to go to a church I researched online, but I went to one that I drove past earlier in the week instead. I sat down, and I knew I was home. I have never visited another church in Knoxville. I have more close friends than I've ever had in my life. And week after week I am fed the Word of God. Two weeks after starting there, I joined the worship team, and I am now one of the worship leaders. My oldest daughter got saved at this church and so did my mother. Oh, God is so good!

One night at Teen Challenge, I asked God for a wife, and I looked at one particular star in the sky and God spoke to me about her. Told me she would be in Knoxville, she would have a son, and that He handpicked her for me.

January 17, 2017 was my one-year clean anniversary. On that same day, a beautiful woman who had suffered great pain and loss, who was an atheist, got saved at Redemption Church. She was beautiful and unique. She was studying to get her doctorate and had never touched a drug in her life. She had the most perfect demeanor. She was elegant and classy. Definitely out of my league, "But God withholds no good thing from His servant." She really liked me, and she had a son. I knew this was the one God told me about. We got married in June 2017. The most beautiful wedding I had ever seen was my own. God loves me and has been so good to me. We live in an incredible house, in one of the nicest neighborhoods in Powell, Tennessee. We pray together and raise our children biblically. We learn and experience God together. We live a life of love and are expecting another baby.

I have never been so happy in my life. My family loves and respects me. My co-workers and bosses respect me. I have a position at a church. I am confident that God will continue to keep me and I will never return to that old life. My Suboxone doctor told me I'd be an addict for life, but I learned that God made me and He doesn't make junk. I am a new creation. I am a child of God. I am redeemed, I am changed. There is hope for anyone suffering or hurting. His name is Jesus.

Chapter 9
It's a Sin Problem

Kevin and Tyler Kulka

Kevin Kulka

When I was around 18 years old, I can remember going to a place called Mission Teens with my church youth group. It was similar to what Teen Challenge is. We would go every three months to minister to the residents. Most of them were welcoming, joyful, and eager to see us and hear the Word. Others appeared despondent, as though they had been through something traumatic. I remember thinking, "Wow, how did these people mess their lives up bad enough to end up here? What have they been through?" Little did I know that many years later, I would be ministered to under similar circumstances at Teen Challenge.

I was introduced to the Lord at an early age by my mother and grew up in an Assemblies of God church, though my father was Catholic and didn't attend church with us. My earliest memories include sitting in the pews singing the old hymns, which were a far cry from Hillsong and Bethel! I was involved in Sunday school, Royal Rangers, and Friday night youth group, which I always looked forward to. I knew the Lord and spent much time in His Word and in prayer. Aside from my parents' divorce, I enjoyed a great childhood. My great grandparents also nurtured me in the Lord and I often went to church with my aunt, uncle, and cousins. My uncle would read and teach God's Word to all of us. I was without excuse for the decisions I would later make.

Growing into my teens, I immersed myself in music, specifically the guitar. Playing in various bands, I fell in love with rock and roll and everything that came with it. I began compromising the standards of my upbringing, drinking beer and occasionally smoking pot to enhance my creativity. When I was eighteen, my grandmother was diagnosed with cancer. I took a few of her pain pills to see what would happen and fell in love with the euphoria. Depression and anxiety began overwhelming me in my early twenties, yet instead of casting my cares upon the Lord, I experimented further with different drugs.

After my parents' divorce, for a while I saw my father on weekends. Eventually he remarried and disappeared, leaving me bitter towards him. My grandmother, who I was very close with growing up, slowly lost her battle against cancer, leaving just my mother and me. I watched her struggle to get by, leaving me very uncertain and fearful of the future. One of my greatest fears was being alone. Watching the family I once knew disintegrate, I began to realize how difficult and unfair life could be. It became hard to trust God and I sometimes felt as if He'd forsaken me.

My life became filled with compromise. During a band rehearsal on a Super Bowl Sunday, I realized I was getting addicted to cocaine. That evening, everything was turning black and my heart felt like it was going to explode. I really thought I was going to die. While being rushed to the hospital, I pleaded with the Lord to forgive me and let me live. My vitals eventually stabilized, and lying in the ER, I swore to God and myself that I'd never sniff coke again. This was one of the first prominent displays of the Lord's mercy and lovingkindness towards me.

In 1990, I married a girl from youth group whom I'd met 10 years prior. Things couldn't have been any better...until my mother became ill a year later. The night she received the medical results, I called her, and she was in tears. I quickly left work for her house where I learned that she was diagnosed with Acute Myelocytic Leukemia, a very aggressive form of cancer. Two days later, she began chemotherapy. The chemo almost killed her. At one point, she developed a weeklong 104° fever. One evening, my best friend and I went to her and prayed. God heard our cries and the fever quickly subsided!

The following two years were very difficult. My wife and I moved into my mother's place to take care of her. I couldn't eat or sleep for a while. I developed severe heart palpitations and muscle tension, leading to eventual hospitalization. Following many inconclusive tests, I was referred to a psychiatrist who prescribed me Klonopin and Prozac. These drugs gave me instant relief! My heart returned to normal and the muscle tension vanished. It wasn't long before I was physically dependent upon the Klonopin being sure to get my monthly refills on time to prevent inevitable panic attacks. I would remain on Klonopin for the next fifteen years. My mother succumbed to Leukemia in 1993. Until her last day, she believed God would heal her. Today, she is with Him.

According to my prayers, the Lord gave me a son three months later. My wife, her daughter, and our son, Tyler, composed a "normal," happy family. However, over the many years, our marriage slowly grew strained. In 2004, we went our separate ways and Tyler primarily stayed with me. I never wanted my son to experience what I had, the sense of instability and loss from a broken family.

During this period, I was recovering from two major spinal surgeries. By doctor's orders, I developed a very extreme opiate addiction (in addition to the Klonopin). My prescription bottles would always be empty long before the

156

next refill, resulting in severe monthly withdrawal. I learned to work and function on these medications, keeping my addiction well hidden from those around me, especially my son. I didn't want him to know anything about what I was going through. I had to be strong for him. I continued to go to work every day at a machine shop, assembling rotors for different aircraft and medical equipment.

Tyler began struggling in school. Diagnosed with many different disorders, he was prescribed the same medication I took, benzodiazepines. I worked long days and Tyler was unsupervised, frequently inviting friends over to smoke pot. I often came home from work furious, having to chase people out who thought my house was a party-house. Our relationship grew strained as I lost control over my son's behavior.

My car suddenly broke, forcing me to take two buses to work as I really struggled to make ends meet. I would spend the forty minutes between buses at a Dunkin' Donuts next to Camden's transportation center. There I met John, who was outside at 4 AM selling Xanax every morning. It was very convenient to buy from him when my scripts ran low. My wages started being garnished because I stopped making car payments, further exacerbating our financial instability. I started buying more Xanax to cope with the anxiety and depression of watching my entire life slip out of my control. I was losing hope, trusting in a pill rather than God. I justified

157

my sin by telling myself, "God understands." In reality, and to my own ruin, I had dethroned God and enthroned myself.

The eviction notice finally came. My son went to live with his aunt and uncle and I went to live with my old youth group leader who had become a close friend. I was grateful that Tyler had a place to go, but I had lost my son and the home I grew up in. I was also grateful I had a place to go, but the accommodations at my friend's house were awful. He was suffering himself from declining physical and mental health, and the recent loss of his wife. The house was very neglected and overrun with bed bugs.

After a few miserable months, I managed to secure a single room rental near my old residence. Tyler eventually moved back in with me and we were abusing drugs together to escape reality. Every week we withdrew more funds we didn't have, accumulating fee after fee. Finally, I was fired from my job of thirteen years for falling asleep; I couldn't hide my worsening addiction any longer. After I began collecting unemployment, my son and I would just wait every week for the checks to hit so we could catch a 5 AM bus to Camden for drugs. Drug dealers got almost all our money, and we were only surviving to get high. When I couldn't afford Xanax, I drank alcohol. I also started smoking cigarettes, which I swore I'd never do. I remember passing out on buses and trains, waking up, and not knowing where I was. Many times I awoke in hospitals, not knowing what hospital I was in.

Through everything, we never questioned God's existence or character. Our miserable circumstances were not God's fault, but our own. We began regularly attending church again to hear God's Word and fellowship with His people. We needed the hope and love we found there.

The unemployment funds ran dry shortly after our landlord unexpectedly died. Following a brief spell at my aunt and uncle's place, Tyler and I ended up homeless in Camden. I was now living alongside the very same homeless people I would help out with a meal or a few dollars the previous year. Those many cold, rainy, sleepless nights were the lowest and darkest of my life. This was never supposed to happen to us. I quickly learned about everything that everybody takes for granted, like laying down in a bed or simply taking your shoes off. I longed for the former days when life was good.

After burning every bridge and experiencing a few cold months of homelessness, we were finally ready to surrender. There was nothing left to cling to; exactly where God wanted us! The clay was finally ready for the Potter's hands. Our Assistant Pastor John had been asking us if we wanted to go to rehab and told us about a wonderful woman named Lucy who helps sends people to rehab. Not many days after meeting with her at a local library, on December 15, 2014, we began our journey to Teen Challenge. I didn't realize at the time what a life-changing decision we were making!

It was best to initially keep us at different centers, so Tyler chose to go to Vermont and I went to Connecticut. Tyler and I parted ways in Connecticut when I got off the train. A man approached me at the station and asked if my name was Kevin. He helped me with my small bag, we got in a Honda Civic, and he took me to Teen Challenge around the corner. After they completed my intake process, I was given a nice meal and shown my room. Everyone was welcoming and helpful! That evening, I was so relieved to hear Tyler made it safely to Vermont. Feeling safe and knowing Tyler was in good hands; I slept like a baby that night.

At the first meal I was present for, everyone stood up and praised the Lord. I thought, "Wow! They really take God seriously here!" It was like living in church, but kind of like the military. Before long, I was sent to work at their thrift store. It felt so good to work again because it restored my sense of dignity. Eventually, they even trusted me to handle money at the cash register. After a few months, they took me to visit Tyler in Vermont. It was so great to see him! He was in great spirits and looked physically so much better! During the visit, I met our Executive Director, Rick Welch. With great sincerity, he shared his testimony with Tyler and me and ministered to us. Upon hearing his story, I thought, "Wow! If God saved this man, surely He would do it for us too!"

I am so very grateful for Teen Challenge and the leaders who came before me. Following our experience and many months of learning God's Word, His Gospel became very personal to me. His love was always there, for He had pulled Tyler and me out of horrible darkness and into His marvelous light. He personally showed me, that nothing is impossible with Him, and the promises I thought were only for others, applied to me. He restored my dignity, my hope, and my joy! Homeless on the street, I thought all was lost, that I'd never pick up a guitar again or have another song in my heart. How wrong I was! I now play the guitar weekly with our worship team at various events and church services!

It is so awesome to now work with my son in this ministry! God has done amazing things in his heart and life! He is truly a new creation, and not the same Tyler. He currently manages the Teen Challenge Connecticut End Addiction Team and I coordinate the affairs of evening supervision. It is such an amazing privilege to see many generations of residents come in, grow in Christlikeness, and graduate to His glory! It is so much more than just a job! I've learned to die to self, my false ideologies, my pride, and my stubborn will and to take up my cross daily and follow Christ. To be a disciple of Christ is to live a disciplined life, yielding to God's will, not my own. In this dying, I've learned to truly live. For the change wrought in our hearts, the glory belongs to our Savior and Lord Jesus

161

Christ! He has done for us far more than we deserve or could have imagined!

Tyler Kulka

I was born and raised in Camden County, New Jersey by a loving middle-class family. My parents and older sister spent much time with me, raising me according to traditional Christian values. They have always been disciplined, hardworking, and upright, serving as three good examples for me. None of them smoked or drank, and as a youngster, I never cursed or lied because of my upbringing. When I first started to do such things, I would feel terrible. During elementary school, I always stood out as exceptional, earning only A's and B's and participating in many extra-curricular activities. Everyone expressed high hopes for me.

Through my childhood, our family regularly attended a very balanced Assemblies of God church, where I was a member of Royal Rangers. I've always understood and affirmed the fundamentals of Christianity including the inerrancy of the Bible, the nature and character of God, the deity and mission of Christ as Messiah, and the reality of sin, even my own. I was always familiar with the major Bible stories and maintained my own independent prayer and devotional life. Even into my teens, I read the Bible and prayed with my father privately, sometimes for hours. I've always believed the

Bible instead of the world's opposing ideologies. However, my love for God was ultimately too superficial, and my love for sin too great. One compromise at a time, drugs and crime would overtake me like a small ember overtakes a forest.

In hindsight, I never truly grasped the heinousness of my sin. I overrated my own goodness and minimized God's holiness and the standards of His law. I thought, "I'm a sinner, Jesus died for sinners, therefore all is well." He was my "get-out-of-hell-free pass" and a means to my own ends. Any worth I attributed to Christ was ultimately because of what He could do for me. Who He is or what He had already done rarely crossed my mind. Insofar as my obedience went, it was that I might be blessed, not that He may be glorified. Though I often prayed for good things, it was typically no more than a spiritual shopping excursion. Furthermore, I ignored the warnings of the Bible or considered them applicable only to others. Finally, and very damningly, I grew to equate euphoria and good feelings with spirituality, believing that good feelings meant the Spirit of God was with me. Comfort and pleasure were really my gods.

I entered high school around the same time my parents divorced and years after our family church attendance had ceased. My A's and B's immediately became D's and F's, and it didn't bother me. Most would attribute my academic failure to the divorce, but in actuality, I was growing too self-absorbed

163

to stress over my parents' marriage. My concerns lay more in the petty details, like how much time I'd be spending at each of their houses. Everyone assumed my failing grades were just a phase. Instead, it got worse. To my shame, I was eventually held back a year. Instead of pursuing long-term goals and fulfillment, I gratified short-term pleasures and desires such as hanging out with and seeking the approval of bad influences, neglecting homework, and skipping school to sleep in. It wasn't long before consequences caught up with me. The threat of being held back a second time and looking like a more of a fool was stressing me out. One climactic day, I suffered a life-changing panic attack. It was so bad I feared I would die. Following that, I never went back to school.

Various psychiatrists diagnosed me with all sorts of conditions including generalized anxiety disorder, schizoaffective disorder, major depressive disorder, bipolar disorder, and ADD. I rejected some diagnoses; however those I assented to, I became a slave to. Like any other psychiatric patient, I had to try numerous anti-depressants to determine which one "worked" for me. Prozac made me very hostile, but Celexa helped my depression. I was also prescribed Xanax, which took a huge weight off my shoulders! It was so freeing, an ecstasy as I've never known! Quickly I became convinced that something was fundamentally wrong with me and drugs were necessary to function. I saw doctors, and eventually drug dealers, as those who could save me from myself. This is where my victim-mentality began, one of Satan's greatest strongholds in my mind. By viewing myself as a victim instead of a criminal before God, I cut myself off from ever acknowledging a need for repentance.

During all this, peers supplied my first tastes of illicit drugs. I was totally hooked on tobacco from my first puff. When I tried alcohol, I realized how well Xanax complemented it. My fascination skyrocketed. My obsession with drugs blinded me to everything I had ever been taught. I called it "self-medicating." This mania would eventually lead me to every other substance: heroin, crack, hallucinogens, Molly, you name it. Each drug became individually special to me in its own way. I had become sinfully, utterly infatuated with the world and not surprisingly, equally apathetic towards God.

Due to years of exceptional respect and sensibilities, theft and manipulation of my family was easy and went undetected for a while. However, arguing with my mom and stepfather was becoming more common, and regular manipulation became impossible. After many fights and my first, and worst, major overdose, I was no longer welcome at my mother's house due to my hostility and unpredictability. I was completely blind to pain of my family as they helplessly watched me slowly destroy my life and toy with death.

My father and I were always extremely close. For years,

he had been taking copious amounts of opiates for herniated spinal discs and benzodiazepines for anxiety after his mother passed away. I never realized any drug abuse on his part. In fact, I thought he had more than enough, so I began stealing his pills and selling drugs. My theft of his drugs worsened his monthly withdrawals. I believe this, coupled with the anxiety of a wayward son and increasing financial pressures, put him in a very vulnerable and helpless state of mind.

Eventually my dad's only car broke, forcing him to take the bus to work. This required a transfer at Camden's Transportation Center, a blatant drug marketplace. When his company abruptly discontinued medical coverage, the prescriptions he was addicted were no longer available and so he began buying his pills at the transportation center during his daily transfer. Our financial state and drug abuse worsened in concert, culminating in eviction and our temporary separation. We reunited a year later, after our individual living arrangements had run their course. However my father and I were now both unemployed.

We began to regularly attend church again because it gave us our only sense of normalcy and hope. The Lord's Home in Audubon became as a lighthouse for us in these dark and stormy days. Were it not for their food, we would have starved. Were it not for their bus fare, we often would have missed services. Our condition was pitiful and pathetic.

When I was twenty-one, we ran out of couches to sleep on and became officially homeless. We migrated where homelessness is easiest, Camden. We were not the city's only homeless migrants; there were so many! Some have been there a long time and have grown fairly comfortable living that way! We exhausted our stays at Camden's homeless shelters. Then it seemed to rain every other night! I prayed for the temperature to dip under 32° so the city would open warm buildings for the homeless to sleep in. I spent some nights in abandoned houses, occasionally being directed out by others who had already claimed it. I spent a few nights in Cooper Hospital, either because I was faking an issue, suffering from near-infected trench foot, or checked into the psych ward following one of my many overdoses.

I accumulated a few shoplifting charges and spent a few nights in jail, a warm relief from the outside. I dreaded prison, but that fear never altered my actions. At least in prison, I could continue to live under delusions of being a victim of something, and I wouldn't have to take responsibility for my actions. I wouldn't have to worry about things like staying warm, acquiring food, getting high, making money, or avoiding police.

Unceasing physical, legal, and financial insecurity, as well as my progressively reckless drug acquisition and usage produced overwhelming paranoia. Getting murdered or committing suicide, deliberate or accidental, was looking more appealing every day. I longed to go back in time and make better decisions or to have an opportunity to start over somewhere. However, my actions alienated those who most loved me and even if someone did trust me and gave me an opportunity, I was the drug's slave and I'd eventually do its bidding to my own ruin.

Despite our sinful rebellion, God mercifully preserved our lives through it all. He used the consequences of our sins to open our eyes to its wickedness and our own personal guilt. No longer could I imagine myself a victim. For too long, I expected God to bless me in my wickedness. It seemed that my knowledge of the Bible had profited me nothing because of my love for sin, though as I came to my senses, it would serve to remind me of the kindness of God. Towards the end of my run, I quickly turned on myself, hating my sin and myself for committing it. I knew the only power great enough to rescue me from myself was in Christ, so I began to pray that my father and I would be saved from the grip of sin. I told my pastor that we were ready to do whatever it takes to escape our present circumstances, even, and especially, change.

He told me to seek out Lucy at a local library on an upcoming date. She founded Faces of Change, a ministry serving men and women with life-controlling issues, particularly drug addiction. My father and I were high and filthy when we met Lucy, who welcomed us and gave us hope and encouragement. I was only able to see the "hope" as hope because of how humbled and broken I was. We didn't want to go to the program she spoke of, but we wanted real change. The only alternatives I saw were prison and death. Lucy and her friends at Faces of Change walked us through the confusion and hopelessness. She picked the program, made the calls, offset transportation costs, provided us with food and supplies, and all we had to do was remain obedient to the process. I was finally ready to do so. We entered Teen Challenge within a week. My father went to Connecticut; I went to Vermont.

Though I neglected obedience to authority and conformity to structure in my teenage years, the terror of returning to my old life drove me to humble myself through the difficulties of Teen Challenge. In Teen Challenge, I often see people tossed to and fro by their many so-called "options." I am so thankful to God that He thoroughly removed all of mine, and I'm thankful my mother refused to give in to my manipulation tactics, allowing me to just focus on the process Teen Challenge prescribed for me.

Teen Challenge taught me the spiritual and practical necessity and value of personal discipline, specifically regarding punctuality, speech, work ethic, and physical and

169

mental exercise. Apart from Teen Challenge's unpleasant disciplinary measures, I would never have overcome cigarettes. Convictions wrought during my Bible studies taught me to forsake theft. One day I was surprised to realize that I had stopped cursing by accident! Nobody around me was doing it for so long that I just stopped! The joy of that liberation has encouraged me even to this day to keep a clean mouth. And in accordance with a transparent life, which I try to keep open for inspection, I abandoned lying for there is no longer any need or profit in the practice.

Teen Challenge supplied real friends I now call family. Additionally, my family no longer worries about my personal safety or integrity and I have a great relationship with my mother and sister again. They forgive me and trust me once more, and I now understand how precious that is. I have also repeatedly returned to Camden to share my story with others. I obtained my GED and rectified my legal issues, which turned out to be infinitely less severe than I deserve! I have been entrusted to manage Teen Challenge Connecticut's End Addiction Team, while my father supervises our center's evening logistics and personnel. We both work daily together to help those in bondage to substances, selfishness, pride, fear, anxiety, anger, lies, depression and hopelessness as we once were. I am also currently in nursing school where I'm earning A's once again, only because of the discipline I've learned through afflictions and grace.

Now I understand that drug addiction is a symptom of a greater spiritual problem, as often depression, anxiety, and general pain-avoidance drugs are. Not to delegitimize some biologically based issues people have, but I personally never had schizoaffective disorder, ADD, bipolar disorder, or incurable depression, and anxiety as the doctors said. I had a sin problem. I never needed medication, but a Savior! I was also never a victim of anything, but a recipient of immense mercy!

The Lord has never wronged or misled me, though I've continuously misled myself. Had God not graciously intervened, my father and I would be in prison or hell today. December 2018 marked four years clean from drugs and alcohol for us both. We came in homeless, helpless, liars, and thieves, yet Teen Challenge welcomed us, watered us, and God gave the increase. We live new lives today. In our preoccupation with sin, God preserved us and reoriented our affections. When idols struggled to reign upon the thrones of our hearts, Christ was providentially orchestrating His own enthronement. I am grateful for how far down we sank, for against the pitch-black backdrop of our depravity, God's boundless forgiveness and loving kindness shine as a beautiful diamond, all the brighter to me. When I was dead in my sins, Christ gave me a new heart, eyes to see, and ears

171

to hear. My sins were so great, yet His grace and power have proven greater! He has taught me the preciousness of His blood and the glory of His sacrifice. To sinners like us, God says: "Let the wicked forsake his way, and the unrighteous man his thoughts: and let him return unto the LORD, and he will have mercy upon him…" (Isaiah 55:7) Christ is mighty to save and more precious than any and all other things! He is sufficient for every need, faithful to every promise, and as King of kings, worthy of full allegiance. To gain Him and lose everything else is to lose nothing and gain everything!

Chapter 10
Destiny and Purpose

Allison Flavell

My earliest memories are of happy times, surrounded by family. I have rich memories of vacations and summers spent on a nearby lake. I'm the middle of three girls and have loving parents, who always did their best to provide a good life for us. We always had everything we needed and lived in a home where we felt love and safety. Although I felt secure in my relationships at home that security didn't carry over into other parts of my life. I was easily intimidated by other children and painstakingly shy. I was held back in elementary school because I wouldn't respond when other students or teachers spoke to me. I remember feeling afraid a lot, and never wanting to be away from my parents, especially my mom. Every time she would drop me off at school or left me with my aunt, I'd cry for hours. It was extremely hard for me to feel safe or normal in any social setting.

Over the years I came out of my shell little by little, but still underneath it all I struggled with my insecurities. After finishing the sixth grade I then transferred to our town's middle school where once again I came face to face with my inner fears. It was almost immediate that the "popular" kids targeted me and began to verbally abuse and label me. I had never experienced bullying to this degree. Most days I would show up late for class because I wouldn't walk down the halls until all the other students were already in their class. This was the beginning of a very hard time in my life, I couldn't understand what about me people hated so much. I had never even kissed a boy or had a boyfriend, yet they labeled me a "whore" and a "slut." All this constant bullying perpetuated this deep fear of rejection. At home my sadness grew and I just couldn't make sense of everything happening. What was it about me? For the next two years I silently received this condemnation and without realizing it, I began to harbor deep feelings of self-hatred. This anger would eventually manifest outwardly in my everyday life.

It was during my high school years that the anger and rage could no longer be stuffed down inside me. I continued to struggle with kids at school but I was no longer trying to be invisible and instead I allowed my aggression to rise and I became confrontational.

Life at home was also falling apart. My older sister was

176

struggling with a vicious heroin addiction and was in and out of mental hospitals frequently. It broke my heart to see my family so shattered. The space between my parents grew as they couldn't understand what was happening. I remember so many times watching my mom cry in silence as she struggled to understand why her kids were in so much pain. The sadness within me grew and came out in anger towards anyone who crossed my path. I would frequently get in trouble at school for fighting and refusing to follow the rules. Around this time, I began hanging out with kids who partied more and weren't all that interested in doing well in school. I became promiscuous, but always felt so ashamed of the things I was doing. Around this time, I discovered cutting. School continued to be a very toxic place for me and after countless suspensions I just stopped trying and dropped out.

In the midst of all this chaos I began dating a guy who had always been a close friend of mine. He was different like me; we understood each other and I felt safe with him. As crazy as my own life was, I was still naive and sheltered in my thinking and despite what I thought I knew, my boyfriend was a heroin addict. I had always known that he struggled with a deep sadness that drew me to him, but never realized how deep his struggle actually was. Despite our love we had a very tumultuous relationship, and as much as I would have liked to save him from himself, I couldn't. One Saturday morning after

177

a bad fight the previous night I came home to find out that he had died of an overdose. This left my heart shattered into a million pieces. I felt lost, angry, and confused and I blamed myself for not doing more or being able to save him.

After losing my boyfriend I fell hard into a cycle of partying, drugs, and men. I was so lost. For the first time I realized that all I really wanted was to feel loved and accepted but real love was nowhere to be found. Though I felt used and disgusted with my life and behavior, feeling somewhat lost, I continued like this for years. Around 2003 I began dating an older guy that I had partied with and a few years later we became pregnant. As soon as I found out I quickly began to get my life back in order. I quit smoking and partying and started to work more and save money. I was so excited to be having a baby and I was sure that this was where everything would fall into place. We bought a home, got engaged and things were really going to work out. I'd finally have a normal happy life. Unfortunately, this was not to be. After my son was born it became more evident that staying in this relationship was not healthy for either of us, so I took my son and moved back in with my parents.

During these next few years as a newly single mom, I thrived. I was elated to spend all my time with my son. I had a good job, I was involved with other moms in my community, and started going back to church. Growing up, I came from a family that loved the Lord, but was in and out of church. I started building a relationship with God and for the first time I began to feel peace and purpose in my life. I did Bible studies, went on trips with members of the church, and was very involved in all the young adult events there. After all that I went through in my life, I began to see change and I knew that it was only because of God.

Things continued to go well during this time and I even started taking classes at a community college. Although I was doing well from the outside, underneath I had never dealt with the deep turmoil inside. I felt that I was still the broken girl, searching for real love and acceptance. Something inside of me grew bored and this was where the slow fade of compromise took me further down the wrong road than I could have ever imagined. During this time I started talking with a guy I knew from work. As we grew closer, I began to detach from church and all that I was involved in. Again, I believed this relationship would bring me happiness, but I was wrong. I would spend years searching for something, anything, to fill the emptiness that plagued me. The sadness that I had once been able to manage now consumed me, I went from one medication to another. I remember always thinking that I wouldn't wish this sadness on my worst enemy. I couldn't understand how people got up in the morning, how they laughed and how they did normal things; when I couldn't even

179

get out of bed. Then my boyfriend and I quickly discovered our similar affection for pain killers, and started using together. This became the foundation of our relationship. I became the addict that I had always tried to save.

For the next few years I was a functioning addict. I held down jobs, but in time that all faded away. Sadness and addiction consumed me, I spent my days sleeping reality and time away. Where I once felt joy and purpose in being a mother, now I only felt shame and guilt. Every morning, I remember my son begging me to get out of bed. But I wouldn't because I couldn't. If I didn't have a bag of coke or some Ritalin to give me the energy, there was no use in even trying. I could no longer function without the right concoction of drugs. At this point it was becoming very hard to hide what I had become to those around me. I stayed up all night and slept all day. I was irritable and angry and blamed everyone around me for what my life had become. Nobody wanted me around. I ruined family gatherings, vacations, and holidays. The truth was, I didn't even want to be around myself.

In 2014, my dad was diagnosed with dementia. The pain and heartache of seeing him lose his mind was more than I could handle. I had always had a deep love and respect for my dad. He never made me feel judged or condemned. He was always there for me, no matter how many times I tried pushing him away. He always reached out to me in my

180

darkest moments. I wasn't ready to face the truth of who I was, and I felt that now I would never have the chance. The dad I had always known, was now gone. My heart felt like it was breaking every time I looked at him. The pain was so bad, I eventually left home to avoid it.

I took my son and we moved in with my boyfriend. This is where it all completely fell apart. I no longer cared to hide who I was or the life I was living. This house became my prison, my hell. This is where I chose drugs over my son, every day. I was a failure, I was pathetic… what kind of mother is a heroin addict? I couldn't even look at myself, I couldn't face my son. How could I look into his eyes, knowing he deserved so much more? It was clear he was filled with a rage caused directly by my inadequacy and blatant disregard for his emotional needs. He hated me with a rightful anger and I couldn't blame him. His emotional needs could never compete with the power drugs had over me, I would choose drugs every time.

Long gone were the days of fun, partying, and a good high. I used drugs to maintain without getting sick. I became a prisoner in my own mind and fear consumed my every waking moment. I became increasingly paranoid and wouldn't leave my room. I feared for my son who was across the hall yet still I could not cross the threshold. I remember multiple occasions I would call for takeout, and after putting down the phone, I'd continue to binge on cocaine and heroin. Within minutes I'd forget about the call. When they would arrive with the food I would freeze in paranoia, taking my son to hide in my room.

During the spring of 2017 I finally reached the end; even sleep couldn't save me from the tormenting fear I felt. I knew it was only a matter of time before my son came in and found me dead. Every night I would beg God to save me, to take this addiction and sadness from me. I had nothing left, everything had fallen apart and I lost my will to fight. Deep within me I always knew God was the answer, the only hope for a way out of this hell. I remember the day I called my younger sister. The anxiety was so heavy it was hard to breathe but I told her everything. She listened quietly and told me I needed help and I needed God. She had also struggled with opioid addiction and found hope and deliverance from her time at Teen Challenge Rhode Island. Knowing nothing else had ever worked, I agreed to go.

The drive to Providence was scary, I had never been away from my son, never went to a long-term rehab. The scariest part was that something inside me knew everything in my life was about to change. I couldn't understand it at the time, I just knew the journey I was about to embark on would be like nothing I had ever known. I walked through those doors full of fear, shame, brokenness, and hopelessness. I would spend the next few weeks going through horrible detox, unable to sleep, or stay in any place for too long. My anxiety was crippling. I will never forget how absolutely terrible I felt physically and mentally. I am grateful I endured it all because, it was in the midst of that suffering, a shift began within me. I was afraid of being in any place with other people, I didn't want anyone to look at me or talk to me. Despite all my fear and anxiety I was met with love by all the women who had been through the same horrible life of addiction. I could tell right away this home was different, this wasn't a rehab or detox filled with hopelessness. This home was filled with joy, laughter, hope, and love. I didn't understand at first, how this could be real. How could someone look at me with love, knowing who I really was and all I had done. They saw me in a way I never had seen myself. They saw the Allison that God created, a girl that despite her past had an amazing destiny and purpose. I quickly realized that I had found what I had searched my entire life for, the only One who would fill and satisfy the depths of my soul: Jesus. I decided early in the program that I wasn't willing to waste any more of my time or my energy. I needed Jesus and I made a commitment to do whatever it took to surrender my life to Him. I turned from all that I had ever known, laying it all down at the foot of the cross. I didn't enter Teen Challenge to complete a program or conform. I needed Jesus to come heal my heart, renew my mind, and restore my life. I realized my need to look in the mirror and take responsibility for the decisions that I had

183

made.

I went through months and months of reflection, healing, and growing with the Lord. I cried every day for months. It was in that broken place I found healing and grew to know the Lord in a more intimate way. I no longer ran from difficult things, but embraced them with God, allowing Him to lead and guide me through the shattered pieces of my life. I wasn't filled with sadness anymore, but joy and laughter. I felt real peace in my mind and had such hope for a future that I could never imagine possible. I became more aware that drugs were never really my problem, they were a symptom of my lack of connection with Jesus. No amount of money, drugs, or sex could fill the hole in my heart. Only Jesus could!

The year I spent at Teen Challenge was the hardest and yet most rewarding time of my life. That year I made the choice to accept and embrace my Heavenly Father, the One who had been there all along. I began to realize I was created for so much more than the decisions of my past. I knew that what I had found would go with me, and I will follow Jesus with everything I am for the rest of my life.

After completing the program in 12 months, I moved back to Connecticut with my family. Now it was time to walk out all I had learned and stand on the foundation I built while in the program. It was the beginning of a new season, another journey of walking with the Lord. I began rebuilding relationships within my family, and reestablishing trust and connection with my son. Although I was back home with my family, I realized I had not had healthy sober relationships with them for so long. The hard reality was that despite what I would have liked, I didn't know them that well, and they didn't know this new me. We agreed as a family to press on and fight for connection. We would work towards relationship no matter how hard or messy. We would honor God's desire for us to be fully restored. I began working, establishing life back at home, connected with local churches and groups that met during the week. I knew there were still parts of me that needed healing so I decided to connect with a local ministry to start inner healing and deliverance. I was really blessed that God continued to bring the right people to help guide and mentor me in this new season. I continued to go back to Teen Challenge Rhode Island and volunteer, giving back to the ministry that saved my life. Every time I walked through those doors a part of my heart came to life, I knew God was birthing something within me that I couldn't quite understand.

I was learning to balance life and relationships better, but there was always something inside of me that knew living at home would be temporary. He was going to call me somewhere else. The leaders that were placed in my life encouraged me to share my story, testifying to what God has done and the hell He rescued me from. I had many people speak over my life, how the Lord was calling me to work with broken woman, who struggle with addiction. I knew there was a part of me who loved the relational connection of sharing the raw truth about the depths of addiction, and the trail of destruction it leaves behind.

Time passed and life was happening and still I felt a pull inside. While relationships with my family were starting to thrive it was a daily battle with my son. It seemed the harder I tried to be the mom he needed, the more he resisted. The reality of all the bad choices I made screamed in my face daily. There were so many days I had to fight to remind myself of what truth was, because it wasn't looking the way I thought it should at this point. If anything, my relationship with my son was worse than ever with each failed attempt for restoration and connection, I learned to rest in the promises of God. He would be faithful to finish what He started. I began to pull back from what I was seeing and feeling, finding peace that God was moving in this area. This would be another chapter to the story of His goodness in every area of my life.

Time passed and God began to open doors in my life. I connected with a guy named Travis at a graduation ceremony. He had completed the program at the men's home in Vermont. Right away I knew there was something different about him. It was so easy and effortless, his love and heart for God were genuine. We shared the same passion for the things of God. He shared his story with me, his heart for working with the men, and how he felt God called him to stay on as staff. We would share our stories of the good times we had in the program, our love for this ministry and how we were given a second chance. I knew in this time God was moving deep within my heart, but still I didn't understand what was happening. I went up to Vermont a few times to visit, fell in love with the beautiful state, and with Travis. I learned more about the woman's home which they had been working on and opening soon. I felt a desire to be a part of this ministry. I was also resisting all that it would entail to actually pick up and move away from everything I had known. I just couldn't see how it could possibly work, yet I allowed God to speak to my heart. If this was His will for my life then He would make that known to me. I went through a process of trying to fight and control how it would all work out, I wanted it all to make sense. I wanted definite answers, but God doesn't work like that. He was calling me into the unknown, where nothing added up or made sense. He was calling me to step out of everything comfortable and trust Him. I stopped fighting, gave up control, and surrendered my future plans once again into His hands. After yielding my heart to His, a desire stronger then I had known started to rise in me. I began reaching out, asking questions, and making my desire to be involved in this home known.

187

The doors began to open one after another, God's hand was all over it. I was offered a position as the first staff member at the woman's home. It has been a hard move and transition. I have come to a whole new level of trusting in God, and realizing my great need for Him. Above all else I am truly honored that God has called me there. He pulled me out of the depths, out of the pit and placed my feet upon the rock. He has given me a double portion for my former shame. My life is nothing like it once was, I am not who I used to be. He has restored, redeemed, and filled me with great purpose to see His kingdom come. I will now get to serve in a ministry where we will see women come in and find freedom in knowing their Savior. He is the God of miracles, I sit here hopeful and confident in the future. I am now engaged to Travis and we are so grateful and excited for all that's ahead. My son and I are connecting in a way we never have. God continues to restore and heal all my relationships with my family. His goodness continues to follow me, and I believe the best is yet to come!

Chapter 11
Addiction Ends With Love

Frank Goodrich

A few years ago while on my way to do some shopping for the men at Teen Challenge Greater Boston, I ran into a young man that was in front of a popular department store. He was bent over, staring at the ground, and rocking back and forth about to fall over. As I walked past him, I knew that this kid was messed up on some type of drug and was "stuck"! I went into the store to make my purchase with the intention of trying to talk to him when I got out, but he was gone! I looked around but he was nowhere to be found. Immediately my heart was broken, I thought that poor kid is hopeless and helpless with no vision or purpose in his life. "Stuck" in his addiction. "Stuck" with no vision. "Stuck" only able to see the ground directly in front of him. No hope, no purpose. I really related to this young man; because 29 years ago that young man was me.

Luke 13:11-13 "and a woman was there who had been crippled by a spirit for eighteen years. She was bent over and could not straighten up at all. When Jesus saw her, he called her forward and said to her, "Woman, you are set free from your infirmity." Then he put his hands on her, and immediately she straightened up and praised God. "

My name is Frank Goodrich and this is my story. I was raised by loving parents, but my family was also very dysfunctional to say the least. My father was a hardworking, blue-collar factory worker from Detroit. He would go to work every day, but also felt the need to reward himself for his hard work with hours and hours of sitting in the bar afterwards. Needless to say, every day my father would come home drunk. I never knew which father was going to come home that day, the drunken happy dad or the drunken angry dad, I just knew he would be drunk. As you might imagine this instilled a lot of fear and abandonment issues in me as a young man and eventually lead me down some of the same dark paths my father had traveled on.

My Childhood

There were a lot of volatile moments in my life throughout my younger years. Every weekend was filled with more drinking and partying that turned into more yelling, screaming, arguing, and things getting thrown across the room! My older sister rebelled at an early age and in her attempt to find love and peace she found herself pregnant at the age of 15. My older brother hid from the chaos and ran away from home at the age of 16, leaving only my younger brother and me in the home to shield my sweet mother from the onslaught of verbal abuse being thrown at her by my dad. On top of the excessive drinking, my father was also a compulsive gambler. As a result of his gambling our family never had any money, forcing us to move eleven times in a twenty-six month period. The homes we lived in were small and never had enough bedrooms for all of us. In fact, I can't remember ever having my own bedroom growing up and I slept on the couch most of the time. I was embarrassed to bring my friends around and usually never told them where I lived for fear that they would stop by. I was extremely scared, anxious, and timid until I got into high school and began playing sports. Sports were my happy place! I played every sport that I could and really began to excel in football, making the varsity team as a sophomore. But then, my junior year we found ourselves moving again, 200 miles north to the little town of Kalkaska, Michigan. I found myself, once again, having to meet and make new friends to fit in. All the moving and dysfunction through those years made me angry and bitter to the point that I vowed to never turn out like my dad. Then one day it happened!

The Beginning of the End

I graduated high school and my football career was

193

now over, I found myself a hurting, lonely kid with a huge void in my life and an even bigger hole in my heart. I went off to college and it was there that I took my first drink. My first drink quickly turned into drinking every weekend, and before I knew it I was totally caught up in the party scene. I was still living at home, going to college, and working full time. I held it together for a little while, but soon I was skipping class and missing work. Then one day at a party at a friend's house, while smoking pot and drinking, I was introduced to cocaine. I also experimented with many other different substances in the futile attempt to fill the void and fix the gaping hole in my heart. My life was spinning out of control. It was at this point I remember looking into the mirror one morning and thinking, wow I am worse than my father. The man I vowed never to become was exactly who I was! Then, one night things got even worse after drinking and drugging at the local bowling alley. I pulled out of the parking lot and was quickly pulled over and arrested for driving under the influence of alcohol. I spent the night in jail and as my father picked me up in the morning I was depressed and utterly broken. I thought my life was over. But far too often when you are an addict and you hit rock bottom you somehow find a way to dig an even deeper hole for yourself. That is exactly what I did. You would think that at this point with my world flipped upside down and in a state of absolute devastation that I would get my act together, but I did the opposite. I continued to drink and live recklessly until it happened again. I was with my buddies on a joy ride in the middle of winter when I got stopped for yet another DUI. I was still on probation for the first offense and now found myself in an all too familiar jail cell. Depression and despondency were my only companions and I became numb and wanted to die. A few days following my second arrest, a severe winter storm hit our area and I decided that this was the day that I would end my life. While walking to the liquor store, no longer being able to drive because of my drinking, there was a truck coming down the opposite side of the road. I could barely make out its headlights through the snow and I thought all I have to do is take a step into its path and this miserable life of mine will be over. As it approached my heart began to race and I began to cry uncontrollably and by the grace of God I let it pass me by. I didn't know it then but God and His mercy saved me that day from selfishly taking my own life. Praise God for His loving mercy!

God's Intervention

My father and mother decided that they were going to escape the hard winters of Michigan and move out to Arizona and so I followed them. I was not drinking near as much at this point and managed to find a good job working construction. Everything seemed to be heading in the right direction and then it happened again! While at the local tavern having a couple pitchers of beer with the guys, I was introduced to crystal meth, and I loved it. Once again the fangs of addiction began to dig deep into my life and I was completely trapped. I began using meth every day and couldn't go day without it. My life spiraled out of control even faster than it did in the previous years of my addiction. I was lying to my family and on the verge of losing my grip completely; then God stepped in. I couldn't say enough is enough and was powerless to stop myself, but God did. While at the local fair and higher than a kite, I ran into a man who God would use to change my life. His name was Jim and he was manning a booth that said "Freedom from Addiction" sponsored by Teen Challenge. He saw that I was obviously high and lost in addiction and began to talk to me about the program. I took some literature and exchanged phone numbers with him. A couple days went by and Jim called me to check on me and see how I was doing and I was honest with him and told him about my struggles. He picked me up, took me to lunch and explained that he was on the board of directors at Teen Challenge and could get me into the program if I was serious about changing my life. The length of the program was scary to me, but I reluctantly agreed to give it a try. There was something different about Jim, he was a Christian. This man, who I just met, invested into my life. He took me down to get my TB test taken and three days later picked me up and drove me three hours to

196

Teen Challenge. On June 11, 1990 I crawled through the doors of Teen Challenge. My life has never been the same!

Hope Lives Here

The first couple days were very hard. I was scared, lonely, and feeling abandoned. I got up on the morning of day three and decided to leave. Just outside the entrance to Teen Challenge was a pay phone that I got on and called my family collect. Thankfully my mother accepted the charges and answered the phone. I begged to come home and almost had her talked into it when my father took the phone from her and said, "Absolutely not son, you have to finish this or you can't come home." Now I was in a pinch, I had left the program and policy is that you can't come back for thirty days and only when you are serious about changing your life. I spent the night curled up in a fetal position in front of the Teen Challenge center. In the morning when the director came in they opened the gate and I followed him into the parking lot. I met him at his car and began to explain my situation that I had left, but wanted to come back and change my life and he let me back in the program, Praise God! Still not fully surrendered I fought the process for a couple of weeks. It was a Sunday morning and visit day on the campus. I was expecting a visit from my family. Anxiously waiting their arrival the clock seemed to stand still, finally visit time came, but my family did not. The staff at Teen Challenge didn't think I was ready for a visit and

197

called my family and told them not to come but no one ever told me. So I was waiting and watching every car pass by and visits coming and going and none of them were for me. It was then that I broke. I remember getting into a shouting match with God. I was crying and screaming "Why God, why? I want my life back, I want my family back!" And all I could hear God say, almost in an audible voice, was ME ALONE, ME ALONE, ME ALONE. I said "I don't want you alone, I want my life back, I want my family back!" His only response was "ME ALONE." I finally fell to my knees and broke. I said "OK God, have it Your way, You Alone." In a puddle of tears I gave my life to the Lord and finally surrendered. I was saved. The Holy Spirit filled me that day and totally lifted the depression, loneliness, and despair off of my life. It was the beginning of a whole new life and the end of a life of misery.

Freedom is Found Here

In the days following my salvation experience I really began to hunger for His Word and thirst after Him. The staff at Teen Challenge was great! They treated me with kindness and loved me. I had a lot of questions about what I was reading and they always took the time to help me find the answers. While reading the book of Romans, I happened upon a verse that really stuck out to me.

Romans 1:11-13 "I long to see you so that I may impart to you some spiritual gift to make you strong—that is, that you and I may be mutually encouraged by each other's faith. I do not want you to be unaware, brothers, that I planned many times to come to you (but have been prevented from doing so until now) in order that I might have a harvest among you, just as I have had among the other Gentiles."

When I read this verse it leaped off the page of my Bible and stuck right into the hole that was in my heart. I ran to an intern staff member and asked him what he thought God was saying to me and he confirmed what I was feeling. God was calling me into the ministry. I was so excited that God thought he could use an ex-drug addict like me. I continued to press into God and His word. I was on fire for the Lord. I began to fast and pray weekly for God to prepare me for His use. I'm not going to say that the rest of my time at Teen Challenge as a resident was easy, because it was not. The chains were being broken off my life and my heart of stone was being cut into a heart of flesh. I battled with fear and abandonment issues and He set me free. I battled with anger and pride and He set me free. I battled with insecurity and the hurts from my childhood and He set me free. God targeted one thing after another. Discipleship was a journey and there were always teaching moments and things that God targeted and dealt with me about on a daily basis. He truly is the Potter and I am the clay to this day.

Lamentations 3:19-23 says

"I remember my affliction and my wandering, the bitterness and the gall. I well remember them, and my soul is downcast within me. Yet this I call to mind and therefore I have hope: Because of the Lord's great love we are not consumed, for his compassions never fail. They are new every morning; great is your faithfulness."

Changed Lives Leave Here

I graduated Teen Challenge and stayed on for a few months as an intern staff member before returning home. I had a tax return waiting for me when I arrived that was just enough money for me to purchase my first set of curriculum for Berean School of the Bible and I began my Bible training. I got really involved at my local church and attended every chance I could get. I finished my first stage of schooling and received my credentials with the Assemblies of God. One day my pastor took me for a ride in his old truck and asked me if I would consider being his youth pastor, and I said yes. All of a sudden I was a fully credentialed youth pastor at my church! God is so good. I continued to have a heart to help those who struggled with addiction and God made a way for us to open a Teen Challenge referral office at my church. God's mercy is so amazing to me. He took me, a hopeless addict and gave me a brand new heart and a brand new life through the vessel of Teen Challenge.

Answering The Call

Over the past 28 years the Lord has afforded me the opportunity serve Him in many different ways. This once hopeless addict, with only despondency as a companion, has been involved in full-time ministry for nearly three decades now. Currently, I am serving as the Assistant Director at Teen Challenge Greater Boston and am the lead pastor at Pembroke Assembly of God. God has blessed me and my beautiful wife, NolaJean, with three wonderful children and two amazing grandbabies, little Luna Lynn and Gianna Bella. They are the apples of our eye and the joy of our lives.

Things haven't been all sunshine and rainbows for me. I have experienced loss and even lost my way for a short time, but the call of God has anchored my life through all of life's storms. The late Pastor David Wilkerson once wrote, "That which is of God will fasten itself on you and overpower and possess your entire being. That which is not of God will die— you will lose interest. But the plan of God will never die. The thing God wants you to do will become stronger each day in your thoughts, in your prayers, and in your planning. It grows and grows!" Teen Challenge was the vessel that God used to breathe new life into me. My life is not my own. By the grace of God it is my intention to give my life fully to the ministry for the glory of God until He takes me home. I love the Lord Jesus Christ with all of my heart, I desire to serve Him and His people with everything that is within me. Truly it is my reward to be His servant. It is my hope that by sharing my story it would be the key that unlocks someone else's prison and that they would experience the freedom that I walk in today! Jesus Christ has set me free, and He will set you free too! Jesus is the proven cure for the drug epidemic. God is Love and "Addiction Ends with Love!"

Chapter 12
Addiction: Chasing the Cure

Pasco A. Manzo, MACM

The cure for addiction is a fleeting thought for the addict and often short-lived. It is a dream with holes of hopelessness. There are countless self-help books, clinics, hospitals, programs, helplines and treatment centers. Their names say it all: Stairway to Recovery, Ulifeline, Riverwalk Ranch, The Recovery Village. Then there are the Do-It-Yourself Addiction Cures and countless others. The addict knows how to chase the urge to get high; in fact, for most the chase is part of the high. I have been around addicts when they are in this chase to get their drug of choice. Nothing and no one will deter them until they have achieved their desired goal. It is a truth, that for the most part an addict wants to be free, but this turnaround can only come when they stop chasing their high and begin to chase their cure.

A Psychology Today article entitled, "Will There Ever

Be a Cure for Addiction?" said, "The complexity of addiction makes a "one size fits all" solution unlikely. When news broke about the development of a so-called cocaine vaccine, many wondered whether this signaled that an addiction antidote was near. Across the globe, researchers are working around the clock in search of an addiction cure, and their discoveries regularly make headline news. But beyond the media hype is a disease as complex as other chronic ailments such as type-2 diabetes." Dr. Sack states that there are three reasons for this:

Reason 1: Programmed for Pleasure

From drinking hand-sanitizing gels to using synthetic marijuana, our society is constantly inventing new ways to get high. When one substance is banned, another quickly takes its place. What drives this never-ending hunt for the next high? One important motivator is the pleasure principle. The quest for pleasure is a fundamental part of being human. It helps us meet our basic needs by pushing us to work towards specific goals. Drugs provide an instant shortcut to our brain's pleasure center. They flood our brains with dopamine and condition us to seek the next high. As a result, our bodies begin reducing their natural dopamine output. With repeated drug use, pleasure dissipates but the cravings remain. Thus, drugs hijack our natural drive for pleasure. Addicts pursue drugs despite the fact that the pleasure they experience from them progressively diminishes.

Reason 2: We Haven't Got Time for the Pain

If we're wired to seek pleasure, then the opposite is true as well. Avoiding pain is an equally powerful cause of addiction. People often turn to drugs to feel better about what makes them sad, depressed, fearful, or angry. As society continues to see increasingly anxious and depressed people the search for a quick fix will remain a powerful impulse. People will continue to self-medicate to relieve their pain.

Reason 3: Drug Use Isn't Just About Drugs

Addiction is an illness that has a strong behavioral component. Those who are susceptible to addiction experience drugs and alcohol in a very different way than other people. Addicts seek the high more, but they enjoy it less. Furthermore, the cravings, rituals, and other behaviors associated with drug use continue even after a person stops using.

Sack, David. "Will There Ever Be a Cure for Addiction." Psychology Today, 18, July 2012, https://www. psychologytoday.com/us/blog/where-science-meets-the-steps/201207/will-there-ever-be-cure-addiction.

With much respect to Dr. Sack, and while I understand his position, the medical field and so many others tend only to point out the complications of addiction and search for new ways to answer the addict, but theirs are no more than old ways with a new face. When endeavoring to seek a real cure for addiction we must learn from the past. In the age-old fight to combat addiction our thinking has to change if we are going to see different and effective results. We all want permanent recovery; people living functional and productive lives without substance abuse and not a temporary fix.

Almost everyone today agrees that drug and alcohol addiction is a disease. It may start out recreationally, simply "getting high" and being accepted by peers but once addiction takes over it is anything but a high. It would be best described as quite a low. Our country's law enforcement, government and judicial system are now focusing less on penalization and more on providing resources for treatment. While the drug producers' and the medical community are continually providing detox drugs such as Suboxone, Buprenorphine, Benzodiazepines, Anti-depressants, Clonidine and Methadone, sometimes it's just exchanging one dependency for another. Some of the behavior of chasing the next high may be removed, however the addict is still not free of all substances.

I am in full agreement for less penalty. I also agree with more care, along with detox medications that can help the addict find some relief, but in most cases these have proven to be no more than a temporary "quick fix" approach. None of us should stop here and settle for this as the cure for addiction.

There are so many different faces of an addict today. They could be anyone from anywhere. To stereotype an addict as an unshaven guy wearing blue jeans and a hoodie roaming an ally way looking for their next fix is quite mistaken.

One in five people who have taken legitimate prescription drugs for pain relief end up buying illegal drugs to kill their pain. They could be a 37-year-old mother of three children who had a recent back surgery and was prescribed oxycodone, an NFL player who broke a bone and was given fentanyl patch, a professional investment broker who started taking Xanax to reduce stress, a nurse whose dentist does a root canal and prescribes Vicodin, or a college student dealing with the stress of exams and begins taking some Adderall.

While driving north on interstate 95 through the downtown area of Providence, Rhode Island I could not help but notice the billboard that read, "An overdose doesn't mean it's over. Naloxone saves lives. Get it in any pharmacy." I had to ask myself if it is really saving lives or are, we just extending the time for what in many cases is the inevitable? Oh, I get it that the person in most cases is almost immediately brought back from death to life, that's why I carry a double dose of Narcan in my laptop travel bag. I want to be ready at any time to bring someone back from a premature death. Please don't misunderstand me as cynical or unsympathetic, I have spent my life helping broken people and it is the furthest thing

209

from the truth. I would use the Narcan in a flash. However, the point I want to make is that I believe our hope for the addicted people we love and care about cannot be sidetracked. The fact that a Narcan injection blocks receptors in the central nervous system and brings someone back to life doesn't mean we are closer to a solution. We just have been given a reprieve. The sad reality is that far too many times that individual finds themselves sooner than later in the same situation again. There are other issues regarding these options, Suboxone in particular, due to the street value people very often sell a part of their prescription or use it to trade for other drugs.

Addiction is so powerful that I have seen time and time again even after a near death experience, it doesn't stop the addict from repeating their behavior. In fact, for some, they are no sooner released from the hospital after they have been injected with Narcan and they are back doing drugs that very day.

While growing up in 1971, I first heard about the "war on drugs" from President Richard Nixon's leadership. Then in 1973, the Drug Enforcement Administration (DEA) was created to replace the Bureau of Narcotics and dangerous drugs. Through the past 45 years there have been countless bills passed by Congress, funds allocated, school prevention programs, initiatives, and new policies. The United States has some of the world's harshest laws and punishments outlawing drugs, yet we still have some of the world's highest rates of illegal drug use. According to data from the Center for Disease Control, in 2017 there were 72,287 overdose deaths in the United States driven by the deadly opioid epidemic. This was an increase of 10% from the year before. The Vietnam War lasted 19½ years almost two-decades of time and tragically as it was the Vietnam Veterans Memorial dedicated in Washington, D.C. is inscribed with names of 57,939 members of United States Armed Forces who had died or were missing as a result of the war. Yet think about the fact that over the last three years we lost more than that to overdose deaths in any single year. That is taking into account the national push for Narcan and Naloxone, making them widely available and as accessible as possible. Most states provide them over the counter and it is becoming available in more schools all across America. Thankfully, the number of lost lives does not include the several thousand reversals of overdoses because of these medications or the number would be much higher.

Yes, those who declare we are in a public health crisis are correct, especially with the continual increase since 1990 of pain killer prescriptions, heroin cut with fentanyl, and all the illegal drugs sold on the streets.

Many years ago, while pastoring a church in North Providence, Rhode Island, I started a "Say No to Drugs" campaign where we printed t-shirts, passed out literature, preached on prevention, and held outdoor rallies with some great success. I was even recognized for my efforts by President George H. W. Bush with a citation letter in combating the drug crisis.

If it's a war on drugs we have been losing the battle. It appears we have lost on every front. I am not throwing stones at those who have tried to save those who are addicted, but it's time to explore and discover a new road to recovery if we are going to change and save lives.

To bring change, lasting change, to have an addict delivered and set free from the power of addiction, we have to address the whole person, physical, mental, emotional, and spiritual. We will have to deal with the behavior of the individual, change has to come from the inside. To tell them they will have to learn to cope with the addiction and they will always be an addict brings no change and no hope to the addict or their loved ones.

Teen Challenge has found the cure for addiction and it has been proven again and again over the last 60 years plus and that cure is the Jesus Factor. That's what this series of changed lives books is all about, telling the countless stories of those who have gone from addiction to freedom. Every one of them will tell you it was a relationship with Jesus Christ, how He gave them hope, loved them at their worst and reached them when no one else could. The One who has created them knows how to fix them. All they need to do is chase after Him. He doesn't discriminate because of color, culture, status quo, language, male or female, young or old, it doesn't matter what city, town or village one is from. He says, "Come to me, all you who are weary and burdened, and I will give you rest. Take my yoke upon you and learn from me, for I am gentle and humble in heart, and you will find rest for your souls. For my yoke is easy and my burden is light." Matthew 11:28-30 (NIV)

When all is said and done the cure for our residents at Teen Challenge New England and New Jersey is none other than a personal relationship with Jesus Christ. This means not only no more chasing drugs but no more chasing the cure because they found it! There are still so many more who need to chase the cure and find freedom through Jesus Christ. Because we offer a Teen Challenge program that is long-term (12-15 months) the necessary time exists to create structure, teach discipline and responsibility, help residents to rebalance their lives, teach them self-worth and value, change their behavior and attitude, teach them skills, help those who need to achieve a GED, receive clinical counseling and life coaching, and learn to rebuild relationships with their loved ones. These are all good things, but without the Jesus Factor it's just a good, long-term program. The proof that Jesus is the answer is found in the true stories within this book and in the lives of those who walk the aisle four times a year at graduation and receive their diploma for a job well done in completing the Teen Challenge program.

If you or anyone you know is struggling with addiction know that God has the power to heal, deliver, and change every person's life who comes to Him.

**Dollar-A-Day
Resident Sponsorship
Program**

An Investment in Lives that Pays Eternal Dividends

As a sponsor, you can be a lifeline of encouragement and support to an addicted person who is discovering God's love and a new life at Teen Challenge.

For just $1 a day/$30 a month, you can help underwrite the cost of a resident in the Teen Challenge program and give a man, a woman, or a teenager in our homes real hope for a promising future without drug or alcohol addiction!

Your partnership will be a tremendous encouragement to them as they are changed by a loving God from the inside out and become loving, healthy members of their families and a credit to their communities as caring, responsible, and productive citizens without dependence on drugs or alcohol.

Call **508-408-4378**
to see how you can become a Resident Sponsor!

Or visit our website: **www.tcnewengland.org**
to pledge your support.

Become a sponsor today and receive an exclusive thank you gift – a 365 Day Inspirational Devotional.

Thank you!

216

CHANGED LIVES

Ten True Stories: *From Addiction to Freedom*

CHANGED LIVES books series is a compilation of miraculous stories of people who were addicted to drugs and alcohol and with no hope. But now through an encounter with God and the Teen Challenge Program, their lives have been changed. Is there a power stronger than the power of addiction? Can you or your loved one become FREE from the control of addiction and live a productive life? Absolutely yes! These books are a must read, the true stories will touch your heart, and give you and your loved ones HOPE!

Book 1

Book 2

Book 3

Book 4

Book 5

Book 6

Single Copy - $15
Any Two Books - $25
Case (34-36 books) - Free Shipping - $350
Get yours today at: www.tcnewengland.org

Book Seven Coming in Fall 2020

Book Teen Challenge

Church - Men's, Women's, and/or Youth Groups
Church presentations including testimonies, singing, program information, and product sales.

Community Drug Awareness Events
Table with addiction information, residents and staff to answer questions.

Social Clubs
Kiwanis, Rotary, and/or Lions

We want to be involved in your community

Contact the Teen Challenge Center nearest you today!

Papa Pasquale's
Sauce for Change

Papà Pasquale's
Biscuits for Change

Italian Lemon, Italian Pepper, and Sabatina's Sweet Biscuits

Syrup For Change
Pure Vermont Maple Syrup

TEEN CHALLENGE

COFFEE
● FOR ●
CHANGE

CHANGING LIVES, ONE CUP AT A TIME

Our Products Include:
Ground
Whole Bean
Keurig Cups
Dark Roast
Decaf
Bulk 5 lb. bags

All Products $10.00

Coffee Mugs
$5.00

Tea Challenge

Our Products Include:
English Breakfast
Green Tea
Peach Apricot

All Products $10.00

Tea Mugs
$5.00

Visit our website **www.tcnewengland.org**
and find out about our bulk pricing!

TEEN CHALLENGE
Vehicle Donation

HELP CHANGE A LIFE AND DONATE YOUR VEHICLE TO TEEN CHALLENGE!

Every car, truck, mini-van, boat, and motorcycle
we receive helps fund the life-changing program of Teen Challenge!

Donating your vehicle to Teen Challenge is simple.
Visit www.tcnewengland.org or call 508-408-4378!

Since opening the doors in January of 2016,
Bloom has graduated over 35 young ladies—teen girls who have found
freedom in Christ from addiction, self-harm, exploitation
and much more through our short-term, 3-5 month residential program.

Bloom has its own line of products to choose from!

Bloom
Teen Challenge New England, Inc.

When you sponsor a Bloom resident,
purchase Bloom Brand products,
start a Petal Group
or invite us to share at your church,
YOU are making a difference

Visit www.tcnebloom.org to learn more about our program for adolescent girls!

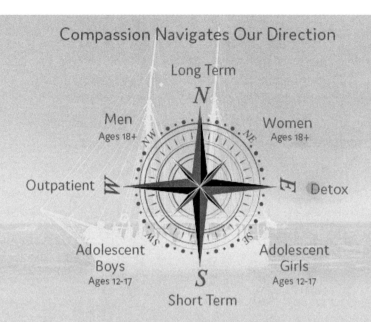

Compassion Navigates Our Direction

Long Term

Men
Ages 18+

Women
Ages 18+

Outpatient

Detox

Adolescent
Boys
Ages 12-17

Adolescent
Girls
Ages 12-17

Short Term

There are three new Clinical Programs in Brockton, MA. Short-term Clinical Stabilization Services (CSS), Outpatient, and Acute Treatments Services (ATS/ Detox).

- CSS will serve 36 adult males with minimal medical supervision and a length of stay from 14-28 days.
- Outpatient is for male and female adults and adolescents with both individual and group counseling options available.
- ATS will serve 15 adult males with medically supervised withdrawal management, intensive supervision, and a length of stay between 4-14 days.

Visit the website at tcclinicalgroup.org

LOCATIONS

RHODE ISLAND WOMEN'S CENTER
572 ELMWOOD AVENUE PROVIDENCE, RI 02907
P: 401-467-2970
F: 401-461-3510
DIRECTOR@TCRHODEISLAND.ORG
TCRHODEISLAND.ORG

VERMONT WOMEN'S CENTER
130 HIGHLAND AVENUE HARDWICK, VT 05843
P: 802-635-7807
F: 802-635-7029
DIRECTOR@TCVERMONT.ORG
TCVERMONTWOMEN.ORG

BLOOM ADOLESCENT GIRLS' HOME
P.O. BOX 603 BUZZARDS BAY, MA 02532
P: 774-300-8070
DIRECTOR@TCNEBLOOM.ORG
TCNEBLOOM.ORG

FUTURE NEW JERSEY WOMEN'S CENTER
NEW JERSEY
P: 973-374-2206
F: 973-374-5866
DIRECTOR@TCNEWJERSEYWOMEN.ORG
TCNEWJERSEYWOMEN.ORG

GREATER BOSTON MEN'S CENTER
54 BLOOMFIELD STREET DORCHESTER, MA 02124
P: 617-318-1380
F: 617-318-1385
DIRECTOR@TCGREATERBOSTON.ORG
TCGREATERBOSTON.ORG

NEW HAMPSHIRE MEN'S CENTER
147 LAUREL STREET MANCHESTER, NH 03103
P: 603-647-7770
F: 603-647-7570
DIRECTOR@TCNEWHAMPSHIRE.ORG
TCNEWHAMPSHIRE.ORG

MASSACHUSETTS MEN'S CENTER
20 CLIFTON AVENUE BROCKTON, MA 02301
P: 508-586-1494
F: 508-586-0667
DIRECTOR@TCMASSACHUSETTS.ORG
TCMASSACHUSETTS.ORG

NEW JERSEY MEN'S CENTER
245 STANTON MOUNTAIN ROAD LEBANON, NJ 08838
P: 973-374-2206
F: 973-374-5866
DIRECTOR@TCNEWJERSEY.ORG
TCNEWJERSEY.ORG

CONNECTICUT MEN'S CENTER
P.O. BOX 9492 NEW HAVEN, CT 06534
P: 203-789-6172
F: 203-789-1127
DIRECTOR@TCCONNECTICUT.ORG
TCCONNECTICUT.ORG

MAINE MEN'S CENTER
11 HUDSON LANE WINTHROP, ME 04364
P: 207-377-2801
F: 207-377-2806
DIRECTOR@TCMAINE.ORG
TCMAINE.ORG

VERMONT MEN'S CENTER
1296 COLLINS HILL ROAD JOHNSON, VT 05656
P: 802-635-7807
F: 802-635-7029
DIRECTOR@TCVERMONT.ORG
TCVERMONT.ORG

Do you have freedom?

Those struggling with drug and alcohol addiction are not free and desperately need the help of Jesus to save them, free them, and restore them! If you don't know Jesus, you too, need freedom from sin and its weight.

Why do I need to know Jesus?

God created us to be in relationship with Him. Adam and Eve enjoyed a beautiful closeness with their Creator, but something tragic happened. They chose to disobey and rebel against God. This caused separation between God and man. All have sinned and fall short of the glory of God (Romans 3:23).

What does this mean for me?

God loves us so much that He sent His son, Jesus, to live a sinless life on earth, and then to die as a sacrifice for the sin that we deserve punishment for. Now our hearts can be made new and we can be reconciled back into a right relationship with God. This is Good News! Will you accept this free gift of salvation from your Father who loves you unrelentingly?
(Romans 6:23) (John 3:16)

Where do I go from here?

To heaven when your life is over! Until then, walk with God, turn from sin, read the Bible, get involved in church, talk with God regularly, and tell people about this great news in your life.

"For Christ also suffered once for sins, the righteous for the unrighteous, that He might bring us to God." - 1 Peter 3:18 [ESV]